T0159910

THE POWER
OF BASICS

IRH PRESS

Copyright © Ryuho Okawa 2020
English translation © Happy Science 2020

Part 1 "The Power of Basics and the Time of Silence" was originally published in Japan
as *Bonji Tettei to Seijaku no Jikan* by IRH Press Co., Ltd., in September 2016.
Copyright © 2016 by Ryuho Okawa.

Part 2 "The Power of Basics and the Road to Success" was originally published in Japan
as *Bonji Tettei to Seiko eno Michi* by IRH Press Co., Ltd., in June 2017.
Copyright © 2017 by Ryuho Okawa

All rights reserved. Without limiting the rights under copyright reserved above, no part
of this publication may be reproduced, stored in or introduced into a retrieval system,
or transmitted, in any form, or by any means (electronic, mechanical, photocopying,
recording, or otherwise) without the prior written permission of both the copyright
owner and the above publisher of this book.

BOOKS
IRH PRESS
New York

ISBN 13: 978-1-942125-75-4
ISBN 10: 1-942125-75-5

Printed in Canada

First Edition

Cover Design: Whitney Cookman

THE POWER OF BASICS

INTRODUCTION TO THE
MODERN ZEN LIFE
OF CALM, SPIRITUALITY AND SUCCESS

RYUHO OKAWA

IRH Press

CONTENTS

PART ONE

The Power of Basics and the Time of Silence

CHAPTER ONE

The Power of Basics and the Time of Silence

CHAPTER TWO
Q&A Session on "The Power of Basics"

Afterword • 129

PART TWO

The Power of Basics and the Road to Success

Preface • 133

CHAPTER ONE

A Lecture on "The Power of Basics"

CHAPTER TWO
Q&A Session

Afterword • 207

The Power of Basics

and

the Time of Silence

PREFACE

As we continue to publish spiritual interviews with various politicians and become deeply involved in political matters, I feel our hearts becoming slightly tainted. So, I decided to compile this book, believing there is a need to put out books of a religious nature every now and then.

When a religion grows large, it cannot be completely separated from worldly systems, so we need to *purposely* and *consciously* carry out our spiritual discipline.

After my lecture, one of the members in the audience commented, "I felt as though my heart were being purified," and I felt a little relieved.

It is easy to forget the power of basics for two reasons. One is that you can easily become negligent of the basics once you are promoted and gain more experience because you have younger staff taking care of the minor tasks for you.

The second reason is that, in the advancement of the machine civilization, you can easily leave behind your "true self" as you constantly chase after and become absorbed in new technology.

Let us, once again, be mindful of the importance of regaining the time of silence in today's busy life.

Ryuho Okawa
Master and CEO of Happy Science Group
September 9, 2016

CHAPTER ONE

THE POWER OF BASICS

AND

THE TIME OF SILENCE

Lecture given on September 3, 2016
at Special Lecture Hall, Happy Science, Japan

1

"The Power of Basics"

That Appeared in My Dreams

An introduction to a religious life

This book deals with a religious topic: the power of basics. I decided to give a lecture on this topic because I felt it was needed. This idea, "the power of basics," may sound a little vague or old-fashioned, but those who have studied Zen Buddhism may be familiar with it. The lecture is on this topic as well as on the time of silence. I believe it will ultimately serve as an introduction or, perhaps, as an answer to issues about "how to start a religious life" and "how to develop a religious character."

Happy Science has now grown large, and since it is a modern religion, we are confronted by current affairs in various fields. We probably clash with a number of secular people in different industries as well. Some of our members may distance themselves from secular issues, saying that they are simply not suited to deal with them. But they cannot always avoid secular issues, and as they get caught up in this world, they might end up losing their spirituality.

There is certainly no such thing as an "almighty talk" that covers all the important points. But I would like to give a lecture on the power of basics because some people may have forgotten about it or may not have even noticed its importance unless I occasionally talk about basic matters.

Two dreams that prompted me to talk about the power of basics

The reason I chose "the power of basics" as the theme of this lecture is because of a real problem I experienced. To tell the truth, I recently had two dreams associated with the power of basics within the past week or so. It was quite a peculiar experience for me.

The first dream happened around three o'clock in the morning. I was confronted by two spirits who appeared to be the *ikiryo*[*] of former executive directors who had worked closely with me. I was being troubled by these spirits, when one of the current executives at Religious Affairs Headquarters appeared in the dream, wrote "Bonji Tettei" [The Power of Basics][†] in Japanese kanji characters on a piece

---

[*] *Ikiryo* is the combination of the strong thoughts of a living person and his or her guardian spirit. It may sometimes wander into various places and cause trouble to others.

[†] Translator's Footnote: *Bonji Tettei* literally means thoroughly practicing what one is supposed to do as a basic requirement. As you continuously dedicate yourself to practicing the basics, you will be able to achieve extraordinary heights in what you do.

of thick paper using a calligraphy brush, and displayed it to the *ikiryo*. Oddly enough, the two spirits immediately turned away and dispersed. That was my first dream.

What did the dream signify? What was the true meaning behind it?

The *ikiryo* were of people who had attained a very high status as a result of working at Happy Science for a long time. In reality, they had not engaged in any actual work and would only give some comments occasionally. In a way, they had been "placed on a pedestal." These people's *ikiryo* were dispelled when a much younger person, who has begun to take on a similar executive role, showed them the piece of paper with "The Power of Basics" written on it.

Ordinary companies and government offices probably have similar issues with employees of a higher status. I imagine there are many workers in a position of seniority who, after being promoted to a high position, have become satisfied with just making general comments from a broad perspective without doing the specific tasks themselves, and making the people in lower positions do all the work. They may believe they have become a great person after having attained a high status, position, or income, but surprisingly enough, it is possible that they are simply moving backward. We should not forget this point.

The people who came to me as *ikiryo* certainly dedicated themselves to the basics when they were younger; they thought it was a matter of course for everyone to be assigned basic tasks and to do them properly. They may indeed have been strict with themselves, but as time passed, they no longer had to do such tasks, and in a way, they may have become "unnecessary personnel."

The problem is that some people do not realize that they are becoming unnecessary. They may think they are providing high-level advice, but the things they say are obvious to all, which makes the subordinates want to say, "We don't need to be told that. Please do your work instead of meddling with us." They might have been transferred to another section under such circumstances, but perhaps did not understand the situation.

The visit from the *ikiryo* is evidence that the two people to whom the spirits belong have a certain attachment to or concern for worldly matters. Since they are not dead, their guardian spirits, combined with their thoughts, came to me to try to express their opinions, but they themselves have not realized that Happy Science was already running smoothly without them.

This was the dream I had. No one conducted any religious ritual like "El Cantare Fight,"* Kigan [ritual ceremony] to exorcize devils, or Kigan to expel *ikiryo*; the *ikiryo* fled after simply being shown the four kanji characters of "Bonji Tettei" [The Power of Basics], which was surprising.

---

* "El Cantare Fight" is a Happy Science ritual prayer to exorcize devils. The prayer is included in *Prayers Book I*, which is granted to Happy Science devotee members.

On a different day, I had another dream related to the power of basics. This time, I did not see any *ikiryo*, but I continued to think about the same theme in my sleep. Thus, these are the two recent instances that made me think about the power of basics, so I thought this was a necessary topic to cover.

2

Common Results of the Power of Basics

Examples of the basic tasks at work

When people start a new job, they always start from the basics. This is true for any kind of job. In society, it is common for new recruits to be given the kinds of tasks that make them think, "I cannot believe someone like me, who has gone through so much training, education, and experience, has to do such tedious work." I imagine this is especially true for young people. Even if they believe they have dedicated themselves to four years of difficult studies and high-level discussions in university, the first tasks assigned to them as new employees can be extremely boring.

For example, the Ministry of Finance once had a reputation for hiring the top students, but I heard that new employees were only assigned to make photocopies in their first year. They would be told to make 100,000 copies of certain documents and not be allowed to do anything else. Even so, they would still get reprimanded with comments like, "The edges are uneven," "Some pages are missing," or "The paper is creased," and were made to redo the job.

In another case at the Ministry of Finance, new employees were asked to come in to work early in order to cut out and post all the news articles related to the Ministry of Finance from five or six different newspapers. I heard that they did just this task continuously for about a year.

Other companies most probably have a similar tendency. The same was true for me when I worked at a Japanese trading house. When I started working there after university, I was assigned the work of reading a large amount of English documents every day. These documents were trade letters of credit, also known as L/C, and my job was to check that all the contract provisions agreed upon with foreign companies were accurately reflected in the English documentation, without any mistakes.

Human errors are inevitable at work, so I carefully read the letters of credit to check each word of all related documents to make sure the content was accurate. I checked everything, including any misprints or typos. I am not sure how many thousands or tens of thousands of these English documents I read. Of course, reading these documents was not like reading books for pleasure; it was monotonous work, similar to proofreading a manuscript.

I now proofread my books in both Japanese and English. Ever since I started writing my own books, I have been told that my proofreading is very fast. In the past, we had an editing company helping us, and they were surprised by how quickly I did my revisions. The editing company staff told me that "Most writers need at least a week to fix their edited work, and we usually don't get the manuscript back for about a month. They have to make many corrections, so the manuscripts are not returned very quickly." In my case, however, I got the manuscripts back to them in about one day, so they were very surprised, and remarked, "How is it possible to get them back to us so quickly?"

Since I spent years working on carefully scanning and checking tens of thousands of English documents for errors, the work was probably not so different from proofreading. While I was in the United States, I even checked for errors in English documents typed by Americans because we could not receive any payment unless the documents were perfect.

In those days, we also drew up bills of exchange for the payment of trade commodities. Usually, the drawers make payments to the drawees, but we drew up bills for requests of payment. In other words, we were essentially buying the documents. Of course, the actual goods were handled by the delivery division. The receiving and the delivery of products from ships were handled by a different division than mine, while I checked the documentation of those transactions. My work was mainly checking those bills and the flow of bank funding. Since payment would not be made if there were any errors in the documents, I worked on those tasks endlessly in my early days.

How I gained the ability equivalent to an editor-in-chief of an English newspaper

Thanks to that experience, I have gained the ability to read books thoroughly. Other people may be surprised by this, but I am able to immediately spot mistakes after a quick scan of a document, even if it is written in English. This is probably the level of an editor-in-chief at an English-language newspaper. I think they also work within extremely short deadlines, and are required to look over the articles written by journalists and swiftly correct any errors. In the same way, I can quickly go through an entire document and immediately spot any errors, spelling mistakes, typos, or inconsistencies. So, when I read a newspaper in this way, I can grasp the overall information after a quick glance.

I do think I did a great deal of very tedious work, but as a result, I am now able to read meticulously. It is most probably because I did these basic and simple tasks repeatedly, day after day.

Moreover, if there were any errors in my work, I had to redo the documentation again. In other words, I had to correct my own mistakes, so all errors would always come back to me. For example, after I checked the documents and created a bill of exchange, they would be delivered to a foreign bank. Of course, the bank would also check the documentation, and sometimes, we would receive a telex saying that the bank could not make the payment because the documentation did not match the contract. I would be shocked by the mistakes I had made, and would have to make all the corrections. If such errors were repeated, my company would lose trust.

The amount of money we handled was quite large, so any mistake was certainly a big issue. The transactions involved hundreds of millions or even billions of yen [millions or tens of millions of US dollars], but since this business was based solely on trust of the documentation, even a minor mistake was unacceptable. I imagine people like lawyers, or people in life insurance or damage insurance, would also check documents with precision and in detail. These professions require extremely precise work. But these tasks are not enjoyable; they are far from interesting.

Another effect of that kind of work was that it made me very careful about managing my health. Back then, it was common for the workers at the trading companies to go out drinking at night, but drinking often caused mistakes at work the next day. That was always a great fear for me, so I made every effort to make sure I did not drink too much. I remember adding a lot of ice to water down my drinks and reduce the alcohol content when I socialized with my coworkers.

Mistakes were always made the morning after drinking; I would miss some points that should not have been overlooked. My job involved meticulous observational work, much like that of a Swiss watchmaker, but when alcohol remains in the body, the brain simply does not work. My brain would work poorly all morning and only get back to normal after eating lunch, so there were always mistakes made in the morning. Even so, I had no choice but to go out drinking with others, so I remember struggling a lot with this dilemma.

Attending graduate school while working at the New York headquarters

I also attended graduate school in the United States [Graduate Center of the City University of New York], so with my studies, I had an extra load to bear. In other words, while I had classes to prepare for, I also had to work.

In graduate school, we used English textbooks and had to cover about 50 to 100 pages for each class. This was an extremely fast pace. But there were times when I had to work late into the evening or get dragged along for drinks or to karaoke after work, so by the time I got home around two o'clock or half past two in the morning, I had no time to do the preparatory reading for class. The other students in class were Americans who read English as their native language, and even they were having trouble doing the preparatory reading. Since the class progressed at a pace of 50 to 100 pages per session, we would finish a thick textbook every two to four sessions. I felt like it was too much to handle.

Almost everyone else took the class as full-time students; the companies that employed them paid for their school expenses, and they also received time off from work to study. In my situation, I had been told to go to graduate school while working full time, on top of the disadvantage of being Japanese. Furthermore, the workload at a company does not adjust itself to accommodate the pace of study at graduate school; when things got busy at work, they were simply busy. And I would also occasionally get invited to go drinking after work. I remember having such a tough time that I almost cried, not knowing what to do.

As a result of my workload, I would sometimes have to go in to work on Saturdays, my day off. I was supposed to have Saturdays and Sundays off, but when I just could not handle all the work during the week, I would go to the 110-story One World Trade Center, which no longer exists, show my ID card, insert it into the security slot, take a big elevator up, and get to my piled-up work on my days off. Since the ceiling lights could not be turned on, I worked under an electric light stand. There were times when that was my only option. Out of necessity, I had to work at least twice as fast as the average worker; otherwise, I could not complete my work. In that sense, it was a very taxing time.

Generally speaking, that kind of work is carried out in a beta-wave state,* so I would most probably have been in a "restless" mood. However, as I continued to do my

---

* There are several types of brain waves. Beta waves are dominant when people are active, such as when they are working busily or meeting others. Alpha waves are dominant when people have a calm mind or are in a meditative state. In an alpha-wave state, people are more susceptible to receiving inspiration from heaven.

work calmly and consistently, I eventually became able to handle tasks at an extremely fast pace. Then, what had been conducted in a beta-wave state was gradually handled in an alpha-wave state; I became capable of getting my work done naturally and smoothly without any particular feeling. This was perhaps a time when I gained greater abilities at work.

Seeing the stitches on a thrown baseball

Mr. Tetsuharu Kawakami was a Japanese baseball player known for his outstanding batting ability who later became manager of the Yomiuri Giants. He once commented that in his peak batting condition, a pitched ball would appear stopped when he stood in the batter's box. Since I am not a professional baseball player, I cannot say I understand this from experience, but I can understand the feeling. It is probably similar to the feeling experienced in Zen; when you are hitting in your best condition, the ball can really seem like it has stopped in midair.

He also stated that he could apparently see the stitches on a ball thrown from the pitcher's mound. Since the ball spins at a very high speed, of course it should not be possible to see the stitches on it. However, an outstanding batter like him will say such things. His eyes are certainly different from those of average people, so maybe he could actually see the stitches. Professional athletes have an excellent dynamic vision, and they have an exceptional ability to track objects moving at high speeds, so they may be able to see things that average people cannot. So, perhaps, he did see the stitches on the ball.

Being able to see the stitches on the ball means that he could see the rotation of the ball—he could see whether it was spinning vertically, horizontally, or diagonally. In other words, he could anticipate where the ball would fly based on where it was hit. Since this was a split-second decision, that may be why he said the ball appeared to have stopped for a moment. In this sense, if you keep training yourself and exceed a certain level of proficiency, you will most certainly be able to perceive a difficult challenge as an easy task.

The ability to see with the mind's eye

There are all sorts of paths in life, but no matter which path you decide to take, you need to go through a certain period of training until you master the basics. This period is extremely important. Those who have neglected this training will develop a habit of doing their tasks sloppily, and will not be able to do advanced work. When they begin to take on various tasks that are slightly more difficult, like decision-making duties, mistakes are bound to happen. This is because they have not fully mastered the basics.

There is a famous story related to this topic involving a German philosopher, Eugen Herrigel, who came to Japan to study *kyudo* [traditional Japanese archery] under a master archer. His experience is explained in his book, *Zen in the Art of Archery.*

Herrigel trained under a master archer, but he did not understand what the master meant by seeing the target with his mind's eye. He could not believe he could see the target with his mind's eye and thought that the only way to see was with his own eyes. He wanted to know the techniques for how to look at the target, what posture to maintain, where to aim, how strongly the string should be pulled back, and the right timing to release the arrow to hit the target. He wanted scientific and rational instruction. But the master did not teach such things, and simply told Herrigel to see the target with his mind. Herrigel could not believe it was possible and almost quit training.

Seeing that Herrigel was unable to understand what he meant, the master said, "Come to see me this evening." When Herrigel went that night, the master shot an arrow at a target placed against something like a white earthen wall with just the light from one incense stick. The target in the distance was almost imperceptible in the faint light of the incense stick, but he nevertheless pulled back and released his arrow.

The master then shot another arrow. When Herrigel was told to go look at the target, not only did he find that the first arrow had hit the center of the target as expected, but the second arrow had hit the nock and split the shaft of the first arrow, piercing through the same exact spot. Herrigel was truly amazed to see how the master had really hit a target that could not be seen, which meant that the master was seeing with his mind.

In order to reach that level of mastery, the master must have undergone extensive training on the basics of shooting arrows; he must have done a countless number of shooting practice exercises in addition to jogging and strengthening his body. As a result, when he reached the level of a master archer, he became capable of hitting the bull's-eye of an indistinct target and even splitting the first arrow with a second shot.

Seeing this, even Herrigel, a foreigner, was able to understand that seeing with the mind's eye was something a person could really do. There is such a book; it is also famous for introducing the spirit of Zen.

Thoroughly practicing the basics to become able to do things naturally

No matter what field you are in, once you reach the level of "master," you will become able to do such things. But this is all the result of the power of basics. In other words, it is important to consistently practice the basics by continuously doing what you are supposed to do, maintaining your efforts in doing them thoroughly, and persevering until you can do them perfectly 100 percent of the time without making any mistakes. Only those who have not neglected such efforts will be able to attain such a state.

In the process of training, there may certainly be times when your physical condition gets worse. Physical exercise sometimes gives you sore muscles. You may also have worries and anxieties for different reasons: Your child may get a fever or be absent from school, or you may be called in to see the schoolteacher; you may dent your car while trying to park it in the garage or have difficulty meeting sales targets at work because of the lasting economic recession; you may have a fight with your spouse, have trouble with your parents, or become a victim of fraud and lose money. There are many environmental factors that affect you and many things can happen in life.

However, you must overcome all these and remain fully committed to the "basics" that are relevant to the work you have to do, although at first glance they may appear tedious. Once you exceed a certain threshold, you will attain a level where you can see a pitched ball stop in midair, see the stitches on it, or hit the bull's-eye of a target in the dark. In other words, you will be able to handle and complete tasks smoothly and naturally, in an almost instantaneous fashion without even thinking about anything. Aiming to achieve such a state is extremely important.

When it comes to work of this world, if you have not mastered the basics, you will eventually end up panicking and run around in confusion not knowing what to do. You may ask someone for advice, but as you hear his or her suggestions, you may start feeling irritated or frustrated, and become unable to stay focused. However, as you gradually become well-versed in your work, you will be able to handle your work unaffectedly and smoothly; you will carry out your work naturally, without troubling others, and you will not even be conscious that you are doing work.

Mastering the basics before moving on to advanced work

The same thing can be said of any path. For example, a well-known Japanese consultant stated that managing a company starts with tidying up and cleaning. As a consultant, he would first check to see whether the factory floor was kept clean and organized, whether there was no trash, nuts and bolts, or pieces of metal on the floor. He sometimes even checked the restrooms. Companies with dirty restrooms have no prospect of success because this shows that the management fails to pay attention to detail. That is why some company presidents get to work early in order to clean the restrooms.

After all, when the employees start losing their spirit to diligently carry out basic activities, their work becomes sloppy and more mistakes begin to occur. Employees may certainly be engaged in different types of work depending on their responsibilities, but it is important to thoroughly practice the basics from the outset to reach higher levels. It is essential to reach a level of competence where you do not need to bother others or yourself. Only after you have mastered the basics can you take on advanced work and become able to handle high-level decisions or take charge of work with higher added value.

Zen temples place great importance on *samu*, or the cleaning discipline, but those who carry out these practices half-heartedly will probably not be able to reach a higher state of mind no matter how earnestly they sit in Zen meditation or study the scriptures.

3

Essential Values That Must Be Preserved in the Advancement of a Machine Civilization

Recent cases of clash between religion and material civilization

Since the so-called "material civilization," or "machine civilization," is rapidly developing and advancing in today's society, we cannot live without being exposed to new technologies. So, it is very important to know how to live in these circumstances.

For example, there are times when working on a computer makes you feel like you are doing work, but it is possible that you are simply spending your day on a computer without thinking about anything in particular. This is something you have to be careful of. We cannot always avoid using machines and computers in the present day, but people who undergo religious discipline must be cautious of depending too much on them because we could lose the true spirit of religion.

Recently, a company that operates an online retail service started a "monk delivery service." Customers can decide the fee, location, and even the monk who will perform the ritual ceremony. Some Buddhist monks agreed to such services and are "delivered" upon request to conduct a memorial service for about ¥30,000 to ¥35,000 [about US$300–350]. Even though they insist that they conduct these services with sincerity, I can easily see how it will eventually lead to the extinction of temple-based Buddhism.

There are in fact aspects of religion that are different from a delivery service. A religious service is not like a delivery service. If a delivery service is accepted as a way to conduct a religious ritual, then the next stage could be to conduct a memorial service just by playing a CD of the sutra delivered by mail instead of having a real monk come and recite the sutra. That is why I have been expressing my concerns that traditional temples are in jeopardy.

I have also read in recent newspapers that some Islamic councils in Muslim countries have banned Pokémon GO, a game developed by Japan's Nintendo, because it goes against Islamic beliefs. One of the reasons for banning it was interesting: It was because the Pokémon characters evolve. In other words, Islamic authorities cannot allow the idea of Pokémon evolving because Islam fundamentally denies the theory of evolution. They fear that children would learn the idea of natural evolution by playing Pokémon GO, which could eventually trigger the collapse of Islam. That is why the game was prohibited.

Another problem involves a cultural element. I imagine they must have experienced what similarly happened in Japan. When Pokémon GO was first released in Japan,

Master's sacred temple of Happy Science was also included as a location where Pokémon characters would appear. So, we complained and had our location excluded. Other traditional religions probably made a similar complaint. Since there were complaints made to the game maker to exclude sacred areas from their game, several revisions seemed to have been made later on. The game maker may have thought it permissible to use any building that was eye-catching, but the game could be a disturbance to the spiritual life being carried out there.

For example, I gave this lecture at the temple, but it would certainly be a problem if a number of elementary school children were to gather around the building to play and make a lot of noise. That is why we asked to have our address excluded. Perhaps this is a problem that comes with machine civilization. While things have become convenient, clashes have also arisen in various places. Especially in an age when people no longer understand the meaning of a "sanctuary," they will only consider how to create an interesting product that will generate money, without any thought of the area being holy or secular. We must be wary of this point.

The necessity of human intervention in life counseling and court cases

Of course, the total rejection of technology will cause the operation of Happy Science to "return to a primitive state," so I know it should not be denounced too severely. I also understand that its momentum is unstoppable.

We experienced the following case when a former general manager of Nippon Electric Company [NEC] joined Happy Science as director general of the secretariat division in 1991. At the time, I used to answer many people's personal questions during the question-and-answer sessions following my lectures. So, he attempted to create software that would automatically generate answers to future questions by inputting the patterns of the questions and answers from previously conducted life counseling sessions into the computer. Looking back now, I am amazed by how he came up with such an idea back in 1991. Even after 25 years, people's concerns never cease, and people continue to have new worries, which shows that it is probably impossible to provide automatic answers through a computer.

This was an issue involving a religious response, but I also saw a similar issue being discussed when I was studying law at university. I once read the following idea in an entry-level textbook called *Hogaku Nyumon* [lit. "An Introduction to Law"]: Law could be regarded as nonsense. From the perspective of scientifically minded people, the penalty fee could be determined simply by checking which provision of the law is violated, just as a canned drink can be selected by putting ¥100 in a vending machine. If this were possible, there would be no need for judges, lawyers, or prosecutors.

We would simply have to determine the culpability in light of the legal provisions, so all we need would be to input the information of the crime into a computer and let the computer decide, for example, "3 years and 6 months in prison." Then it would not be necessary for any person to be involved.

As if to give an excuse for the previous statement, the text explained further: Some people state such opinions, but in reality, things are not so easy. Human intervention—a defending lawyer posed against an accusing prosecutor arguing to the best of their abilities, and a judge closely examining the statements of both sides to determine the best conclusion from the perspective of the law—will always continue to exist.

I remember this from my studies. The point is that people have a tendency to desire tools or methods that always yield the same results no matter who does the procedure. However, no single trial proceeds in the same way as another. This is because human activity is involved and the act of "thinking" comes into play.

When a verdict cannot be decided, a jury will be involved in some cases and their judgments will be heard. If the case is serious, like one involving the death penalty, a jury is consulted. Such procedures are sometimes necessary because the verdict could be unjust if the judge's views on life were biased. While I do have some concerns about such things, I am not necessarily denying modern technology in its entirety.

Excessive use of computers can lower your intelligence

From my own experience, there is an episode involving my ex-wife. In the past, after I gave major lectures consecutively, she would take me on trips to the islands in Southeast Asia to help me recharge. We usually stayed for about a week, taking with us books that we would not normally read. I would take a difficult book by William James,* for example. In other words, I would take books that I normally would not read or those that required much time to get through. I would take the time to carefully read these books while on the trips before returning home.

As for my ex-wife, she would take books like Montaigne's† *Essays* and just spend her time reading in the island hotel. There was such a time in our lives. Even though she did not read as much as I did, at one point, she probably read over 300 books in a year.

In those days, when we took walks together, we would have intellectual discussions. Our walks were just like the painting of Plato and Aristotle walking and talking [*The School of Athens*], in which Plato points to the heavens while Aristotle holds his hand out with his palm facing down. This

---

* William James (1842–1910) was an American philosopher and psychologist. He taught pragmatism, which places emphasis on utility. His notable works include *Pragmatism* and *The Varieties of Religious Experience*.

† Michel de Montaigne (1533–1592) was a French philosopher and moralist. He is famous for his work *Essais* (Essays), which was written based on his abundant knowledge of and insight into human nature.

painting depicts the "Peripatetic school" in which students deepened their philosophical understanding by having discussions while walking. We really held deep philosophical discussions as we walked.

I think it was around 2006, when stock prices were beginning to go up, that my ex-wife began day trading. At the time, it was popular to buy and sell well-known stocks on the computer while being at home, and she apparently happened to see an actress she knew commenting in the Sunday newspaper that she, too, did day trading. This stimulated my ex-wife's sense of rivalry, prompting her to take up day trading on the computer.

However, she soon became absorbed in using the computer. Not only did she buy and sell stocks, but she also started buying other things online. Eventually, products began arriving at our house every day. And so, just like the stories commonly heard, she became somewhat addicted, sitting in front of the computer all day, and stopped reading books.

In less than a year, we started running out of topics to discuss whenever we talked. Although in the past we had been able to walk and talk in a similar form to the Peripatetic school tradition, we were no longer able to hold deep conversations. Old books like Montaigne's *Essays*, for example, are probably boring to most people because the content no longer applies to modern times and are most likely of no use in conversation now, but my ex-wife was the kind of person who would read such classics. But when she learned how to use the computer and began to spend her day just surfing the Internet, her enthusiasm for shopping online caused her to stop reading books, and we could no longer hold meaningful conversations together.

Furthermore, from around that time, she started to make extremely shallow decisions at work. Just as computer codes are made up of zeros and ones, her decisions became very simple, and her opinions started to differ greatly from mine. Thinking about it, I could say that reading various books has an effect on the formation of wisdom. She herself probably did not believe that her intelligence had deteriorated. Rather, she may even have believed that she had gotten wiser than before because she could now use a computer to look up all sorts of information and buy a variety of goods. However, I personally got the impression that she became less intelligent in about a year's time.

Furthermore, she began to make poor managerial decisions and frequently took the complete opposite position from mine. She insisted that she could not be wrong because she was being progressive, but from the perspective of someone who had thoroughly read many books on management, I often found that her decisions definitely went against basic rules of management. She started to make decisions in a reflexive manner, frequently responding to situations in an animalistic way and causing many problems. Perhaps such incidents could provide a basis for a husband and wife to start differing in their ways of thinking.

A strange experience while giving a lecture

Recently, my second son published a book that included a lecture he had given at Happy Science University [HSU] in Chiba Prefecture on an ideal lifestyle of a student. The lecture was given in a large tiered room, the kind where the speaker feels as if he or she is at the "bottom of a large pot." Everyone looks down from above, so it is a slightly uncomfortable place to speak. But since it was the largest classroom at HSU, he used it for the lecture.

In the lecture, he explained his ideas using a PowerPoint presentation and displayed charts to make it easier for the students to understand. He introduced three different ways students A, B, and C attending various universities could spend each day. He thus explained, by PowerPoint, the ideal way to spend a day and week.

However, according to what he told me after giving the lecture, he felt that something had left his body and his energy was suddenly gone as he was using PowerPoint to explain his ideas. He said that he felt weak and could no longer emit heavenly vibrations. He was saying things a psychic medium would say, but I think it is possible for something like this to happen.

A guiding spirit had most likely been with him to support him in his lecture, but I assume that it left the moment he touched the computer. This is totally understandable. Since PowerPoint did not exist 100 years ago, the guiding spirit was probably bewildered by the new tool, did not know what to do, and immediately left him. I found it very interesting to hear how his energy was drained.

In the Bible, there is a passage that describes Jesus feeling his energy suddenly leaving his body as he passes through a crowd. A woman who had suffered from bleeding for years said to herself, "If I only touch his garment, I will be made well," and touched the fringe of his garment. Perhaps because spiritual energy flowed from Jesus, the woman was healed, but at the time, Jesus said, "Someone touched me, for I perceive that power has gone out from me." There is such a scene in the Bible, and what my son experienced may have been similar to this. He described such an experience.

Because of machines, our lives today have certainly become convenient in many ways, so I do not think we should deny modern technology entirely. For example, I do not think we should replace room lights with candles, nor would I recommend fishermen who catch fish with large nets to go back to using fishing rods or harpoons to spear fish. However, you need to know that the advancement of material civilization can cause you to lose sight of the essence of your work depending on your occupation.

As I mentioned earlier, based on a worldly understanding, it may be impossible to shoot an arrow in the dark night and hit the bull's-eye. In this modern age, people may use an automatic rifle and the like to hit a target, so such an exquisite skill may not always be practical. But I do think mastering such a skill is one possible way of life.

When religious leaders attend to people's anxieties and worries, there may be a similar aspect to hitting the center of a target with an arrow in pitch black. Our perception is limited in the darkness; we can only see people's facial expressions through our eyes and hear their voices through our ears. But there are times when religious leaders can intuitively and instantaneously perceive the heart of the problem causing a person to worry or the possessing spirit that is bothering a person without relying on those senses. Humans inherently have such abilities, but as we become constantly engaged in completely different tasks, our intuition can gradually become less accurate and less sensitive. This is something we should bear in mind.

Making sure the basics are not neglected in the process of evolving

Since the world is developing rapidly, changes inevitably occur within religion and in the spiritual discipline as well. When giving lectures, I also use convenient tools like satellite broadcasting and devices that convert my lectures into DVDs and CDs. These tools allow me to reach a great number of people in a year—a number that someone living in the olden days would have had to spend a whole lifetime to achieve. We have entered such an age. However, just like in the saying "Ploughing the field and forgetting the seeds," we must be careful not to lose the "soul of work."

For example, Buddhist monks put much effort into creating a posthumous Buddhist name using kanji characters to be given to a deceased person. They used to receive large fees of about ¥1–4 million [about US$10,000–40,000] to create such names, but since people today are becoming weaker in kanji characters, it has become more difficult for monks to think of posthumous names.

To solve this problem, convenient computer software that produces appropriate posthumous names has now been developed and sold. The names are produced based on information input about the deceased person, such as personal history, academic background, and occupation. With the use of such software, the price of a posthumous name has gradually dropped to ¥300,000 or even ¥100,000 [about US$1,000–3,000]. Although there may be some merit in using such software in that it has reduced the monks' burden, it has significantly deprived the appreciation for spiritual value. I believe we must not forget the "heart" of the profession.

The same can be said of cooking as well. For example, there must be a tremendous amount of intangible know-how that a chef learns from over a decade in the culinary discipline. Some dishes can certainly be made by machines, but the question is whether ¥100 [about US$1] sushi made by a machine and sushi made by a professional sushi chef that may cost as much as ¥10,000 [about US$100] are the same or not.

Of course, as research advances, the quality of machine-made sushi will get closer to sushi made by hand. Apparently, there has been scientific research on how sushi rice is shaped by hand, and it has been shown that there is a difference in the perception of taste depending on how much space there is between each grain of rice. As more efforts are being made to improve the machines, it seems like the quality of machine-made sushi is catching up to that of professional sushi chefs.

Moreover, regarding the board games of *go* [a checker-like game] and *shogi* [Japanese chess], we sometimes see master players losing to computer programs. Therefore, we cannot simply rejoice at the advancement of such technology. Please be aware that, depending on the profession, certain jobs can face the danger of extinction, and there is the possibility that a truly important value will be forgotten and lost.

When living in an "advanced" world, people tend to start neglecting the task they must naturally do, the mundane tasks, or the basic work that is considered boring. However, it is extremely important to do such ordinary, basic work thoroughly, and to continue doing it diligently every day. It will help to stop your abilities from deteriorating and to continuously hone your intuition.

"A day without work is a day without food"

There is a story about Chinese Zen Master Baizhang Huaihai. Even after turning 80, Master Baizhang would carry farm tools, such as a hoe and a plow, and go out to work in the fields. On seeing this, his disciples were worried about their aging Master and pleaded with him to stop doing so, but the Master would not stop.

One day, the disciples decided to hide the farm tools from the Master. The Master then stopped eating food and began to fast. The troubled disciples now begged him to eat something, but he refused. When the disciples asked why, Master Baizhang responded with the famous saying, "A day without work is a day without food," meaning, "Since I did not work today, I cannot eat food."

There is another similar expression: "He who does not work, neither shall he eat." This story illustrates Master Baizhang's belief that someone who has not done any work in particular, wasting a whole day in this world, does not deserve to eat, even if the person has reached old age.

So, even if you may find it boring, it is extremely important to keep fulfilling your role in the world in the cycle of everyday life, all the while training yourself and preventing yourself from becoming weak. We must never forget this attitude.

4

The Balance between
Quantity and Quality in Reading

How to narrow down, choose, or discard books

The concept of reading has been largely changing nowadays, but having been an avid reader since my younger days, the best thing about reading was that I could transcend or become detached from worldly matters when I was absorbed in a book. When reading a book, you can forget about the world, your troubles, or things that happen at work, and retreat into your own world. In this sense, I believe there was meaning in reading books thoroughly and deeply for me.

When I was a student I did not have much money, so I read almost every single book I bought. I usually read them from cover to cover, and would hardly leave any book only partially read. Because of this, I clearly remember the contents of the books I read in my youth. Even when I started working, my income and free time were still limited, so I struggled greatly with choosing the kinds of books to buy and the time of day I could spare to read them. I did this until I was about 30 years old, and I believe what I studied in those days laid the foundation for me later on.

After that, I became engaged in work that involved reading and publishing of many books. I now have the financial strength that allows me to purchase a large number of books, so I read books on a variety of subjects for reference or for research. I do this partly out of necessity. I need to be informed about a variety of things, so I read different newspapers, including English ones, and purchase a lot of books that cover even miscellaneous topics. I also watch various TV programs and news to gain necessary information. Since we make movies, I watch different kinds of films as well. The buildup of various bits of information has thus become large in quantity.

When you start dealing with large amounts of information, your intellectual quality is highly likely to be spread thin. It is extremely important to deal with large quantities of information quickly, but there is also the danger of the quality dropping, so you need to be cautious of this.

Young people usually cannot buy many books because they do not have money or space to put them. When such limitations start to increase, you will have to consider which books to choose and which to discard. You will need to make certain choices. For example, you can take a different approach depending on a book's function. Some books are worth reading slowly and thoroughly, while others require reading repeatedly to fully master the material. Some books might be useful just to skim through to grasp the general idea, while other books may not be necessary now but will become useful in 5 to 10 years. There are different types of books, so you should not read them all in the same manner.

So, to lead an intellectual life, you need to consider how to maintain enough inner space to read books as life's pleasure and to prevent the quality of your reading experience from dropping. If you read books for your work, you must also consider whether your reading leads to an increase in intellectual productivity. You need to have these perspectives as a measuring stick to decide how to narrow down, choose, or discard books.

Used books tinged with a will or the previous owner's thoughts

Nowadays, many people probably buy their books through Amazon [an online shopping website]. I myself often decide what I am going to buy by looking at newspaper advertisements. In the past, there was a time when I would actually go to a bookstore and purposely search for books to buy. But now I rarely buy books in bookstores, and since I cannot tell if a book is good or not until I actually have it and read it, I often end up buying books I do not need.

In my student days, I was still able to pick out, buy, and read used books from the used bookstore, but after gaining the ability to communicate with the spirit world, I somehow can no longer read such books. Perhaps it is because I have become spiritually sensitive; sometimes I sense the will imbued in the book, much like the will imbued in objects sold in secondhand stores, and occasionally perceive the thoughts of the previous owner.

What is more, since old books have stains and a lot of microscopic organisms on them, my skin starts to feel very itchy as I read them. I did not get this kind of reaction in my youth, but now I can feel the tiny creatures crawling on me. I am not really sure if this is also because of my spiritual power, but I suspect that it is. I can sense the microscopic organisms. They are also living creatures, so I can sense something from them. For this reason, I have become unable to read used books, which has had a negative effect on my intellectual life.

There are some good books among the used ones, and when I cannot obtain such a book in new condition, I have no choice but to order a used one. In that case, I have my secretary copy the pages and bind them into book form. I feel bad for creating additional work, but with a copied version, at least things like stains and mites can be avoided. There are times when I request to have this done.

Visits from spirits of dead authors

Sometimes even the copied version of a book can give me a bad feeling, and that is most likely when I am visited by the spirit of the deceased author. I have my own book storage in a place about 200 kilometers [about 125 miles] from my current residence. It is no longer where I live, but I keep a large collection of books there. About 10 years ago, I had the entire works of Seicho Matsumoto* sent to me from that storage place because I thought I needed to study malevolence and criminal behavior and do a little more research on evil as a religious leader.

To conduct my research, I decided to read the autobiography of his life because I thought it would be a good place to start. But before I could even finish half of it, the spirit of the author himself appeared before me, and I was troubled by this. At Happy Science, we once recorded his spiritual message, in which I reconfirmed that I could not read his books. I wanted to study more, but it was hard to concentrate on reading when his spirit appeared and lingered. He is read by many others, but perhaps he has nowhere else to go.

As a result of frequently writing crime novels, I presume his mind had become attuned to the world where criminals would go after death. This would be a natural consequence if one deals only with these kinds of themes in writing books.

---

* TF: Seicho Matsumoto (1909–1992) was a Japanese writer who wrote a number of historical novels and non-fiction books. He is especially famous for his mystery and detective novels.

Even if his heart had grown dark, he probably considered it normal. If that was the case, it would be no surprise that he went to the same world as criminals do after death. Although he was a great author in this world, an immensely high income earner, and a diligent worker, I simply cannot read his books.

The afterlife of Buddhists or religious scholars who did not believe in spiritual matters

I also bought a complete collection of the works of Hakuju Ui, who had taught the Buddhist scholar Hajime Nakamura. They were valuable, thick used books, but I could not read them no matter how hard I tried. He was an honorary professor at the University of Tokyo and an immensely distinguished scholar who had even received awards like the Order of Culture in Japan. But no matter which part of the collection I tried to read, he kept appearing, so I simply could not read it.

He was the primary instigator responsible for misleading Japanese Buddhism. With his understanding of ancient languages like Sanskrit, he researched Indian Buddhism from literary and archeological perspectives and established Japanese Buddhist studies based on the idea that the oldest materials are the closest to the truth. This man was the teacher of Hajime Nakamura.

Ui completely denied the soul. He upheld the idea that "Various mysterious phenomena are all nonsense; they are like common ploys used by new religious groups. Miracles are merely exaggerated stories, and there are no such things as miracles. Spiritual aspects must all be omitted." He then created the foundation of Buddhist studies using linguistic analysis, based solely on what has remained of archeological and historical materials or documents. But this has resulted in a completely materialistic and atheistic understanding of Buddhism.

He did not commit any crimes in a worldly sense; he lived as a scholar and was highly respected. Even so, he has fallen to hell. In fact, he could be described as a "learned fool"; although he studied Buddhist scriptures, he did not understand Buddhism. Even after having studied Buddhism, he was convinced that Shakyamuni Buddha taught atheism and materialism and denied the spirit and soul, so he avidly pursued such ideas alone.

A similar tendency was observed in Hideo Kishimoto, a religious scholar and honorary professor at the University of Tokyo. Having studied religion at Harvard University, he became famous in the field of religious studies after returning to Japan. He also served as the head of the University of Tokyo Library System, but later died of cancer. His "enlightenment," attained from his study of religion, was that it is essential to live one's life to the fullest until the arrival of one's death.

He earned the respect of many people, but despite having studied religion, he lived without the slightest belief in anything spiritual, including the other world and the soul. Ultimately, he valued his intellect and worldly knowledge more than anything else, and tried to understand religion only intellectually. Those who have lived in this way would not be able to explain where they are after returning to the other world. They cannot even understand why they exist. This is the ultimate consequence of the study of religion that has lost its soul.

5

A Buddhist Story:

"Drawing Water with a Bottomless Bucket"

Spirituality must not be lost

Returning to my main point, what I mean to say is this: As long as we live in this world, we cannot escape the material civilization, or machine civilization. Technologies continue to advance, so we have no choice but to use them to a certain extent. However, there are issues of "spirituality," "the mind," and "the soul" that must never be lost in such an environment. We must not progress in the direction where we turn our eyes away from these values. Please know that you could be making a mistake if you believe you have attained a richer life, higher income, or more productivity solely through material or machine civilization.

The second point I would like you to understand is similar to the criticism I just made about the extreme dependence on the machine or material civilization. As long as we live as human beings with physical bodies, we will always have inconveniences and limitations in our lives and in doing various tasks. But if we remove all these inconveniences, neglect the basic tasks that arise every day, and just regard them as a waste of time and energy, then we could ultimately bring ruin to ourselves.

In other words, just like in the saying "A day without work is a day without food," you could end up becoming an unproductive person. You may believe that you are engaged in a higher level of work or important decision-making duties, or that you are earnestly pursuing inspiration, but in reality, you may have become nothing. You could be melting away like ice cream in the summertime, turning into liquid and leaving nothing behind. Such things can happen. So, please do not forget that there are important aspects in the specific work you do every day or in your way of life.

Continuous study to maintain your English skills

A young person who had just graduated from university once asked me why I still keep studying English. This person apparently thought I had basically completed everything that could be done in studying English, since I had already given many lectures in English, published those lectures, and have even put out 200 to 300 English textbooks on vocabulary, grammar, and reading. Perhaps this is how it might normally appear to people. However, just as the saying "A day without work is a day without food" suggests, without continued study, one's English skills would only decline. Young people may not understand this yet.

The world is full of putrefying bacteria; many things decompose every day. Houses break down, wood rots, and flowers wither and return to soil. We are living in a world governed by what is called the "law of entropy," in which everything deteriorates, becomes reduced to simpler substances, and returns to its origins.

Even if you studied English in the past, you cannot remain good at it for a long time because you gradually forget it. Even schoolteachers who once studied to acquire a certification will naturally become unable to teach the subject of their expertise if they have not taught for several decades.

A possible outcome of the Meiji Restoration

Even now, I continue to add steadily to the series of *Kuro-Obi Eigo* [lit. "Black Belt in English," published by Happy Science] on a daily basis. I think it to be foolish at times, but I have been working on the series for almost a decade now. The books I create will of course remain as English textbooks, but as I continue to put them out, I strive to maintain my English ability and also try to learn new words and expressions. In addition, there is naturally a benefit to repetition; by doing something repeatedly, you can prevent your abilities from fading.

When Ryoma Sakamoto* died in an attack at the Omiya Inn, he was 33 years old. But if the attack had occurred at age 23, when he was the assistant master of the Chiba Dojo, he might have not been killed. According to author Ryotaro Shiba, the Chiba Dojo [Genbukan] was one of the three major dojos in Edo [Tokyo], so Sakamoto was probably one of the three best swordsmen in Edo at the time. With that skill level, he would have had enough time to fight back even if he were having a birthday meal, because he would have intuited the situation from the sounds of the intruders coming up the stairs and fatally slashing the lookout, Tokichi. Then, there is a chance he could have grabbed his sword from the alcove and met them in combat just in time.

However, at the time of his assassination, a decade had already passed since his training days at the dojo. Sakamoto, the head of Kaientai [a trading and shipping company and private navy he founded], was dining with Shintaro Nakaoka, the head of the military group Rikuentai, when he heard a loud noise. He yelled, "Be quiet!" and continued eating; that is when he was attacked and killed. Even though he was a strong swordsman, it was natural for his skills to have declined since he had not done sword training for a decade. Since these things can happen, keeping up one's training is certainly important.

---

* TF: Ryoma Sakamoto was a Japanese samurai who played a central role in launching the Meiji Restoration to start the modernization of Japan in the 19th century.

Advancing bit by bit

Right now, I am learning languages besides English, but since I only study a little at a time, it feels like I am forgetting more than I am learning and advancing. It is just like the proverb that says, "Drawing water with a bottomless bucket."

When I was in elementary school, there was a well behind our old wooden school building, and I remember seeing a bucket used at the well. In the old days, people would lower a bucket tied to a rope on a pulley system to draw water out of the well.

There is a story in Buddhism called, "Drawing water with a bottomless bucket." You cannot draw any water from a well if the bucket has no bottom. But there would be some water droplets on the surface of the bucket when you pull it up, and you could still gather those droplets into a barrel a few drops at a time. If you repeat this several hundred times, you can eventually fill the barrel with water. There was a Japanese monk in the post-war period who would tell this story. He apparently devoted his life to this single concept.

From this story, I feel the transience of human effort and how progress is made only a little at a time. When studying the *Tripitaka* [the complete collection of Buddhist scriptures], it sometimes feels like one's efforts are as futile as counting the grains of sand of the Ganges River. The same is true when you undergo spiritual discipline on the road to Buddha; it may feel like you are endlessly trying to draw water from a well using a bucket with no bottom, collecting just the water droplets to fill a barrel little by little.

To put it another way, while the essence of Buddhism is to save all humankind, there are billions of people living in this world. Christianity and Islam each have one to two billion followers, and as you aspire to save people by engaging in religious activities, you will find that there are always more people you cannot save than people you can. While you are trying to save people, others will also keep dying, so no matter how hard you try, your goal will always be beyond your reach. Even so, by continuing to do your work repeatedly, you are actually advancing little by little. Please be aware of this.

As you carry out the basics, you may feel like you are acting in vain. However, if you keep practicing the basics, you can move forward a little. And by repeating the basics, I am sure that, in a way, you are preventing yourself from becoming something you are not.

6

Encouragement to Live a Zen Life

in the Modern World

The importance of having a time of silence

This lecture also covers the theme of a "time of silence." You can have a time of silence while reading a book as well. This is an effective way in the modern era.

Buddhism teaches *Zazen* [Zen-style meditation] and other methods of meditation, but normally people may find it difficult to practice it. People living in modern society have many concerns regarding their work, personal relationships, and other miscellaneous matters, so even if they were to get away from work and practice meditation, they would constantly be distracted by such things. As a result, their meditation will often end up being a waste of time.

For this reason, I recommend reading as a modern practice. As you tackle an important, valuable book and read it thoroughly, you can sometimes become attuned to the author's lofty state of mind, if the author is a respectable figure. If the author has already passed away and returned to a good place in the heavenly world, you can find time to be in tune with their heavenly vibrations.

Usually, there are probably not many highly respected people among one's friends and in one's environment; most are probably normal people of this world. We must also interact with all kinds of people, regardless of whether they are headed to heaven or hell. However, among the authors who have written books that have been received as "good work," there are many wonderful people whom we can no longer meet. Making time to connect quietly with such writers will also serve as an opportunity to receive spiritual guidance, though this may sound like an occult experience.

After all, without a time of silence, you can neither become spiritual nor start communicating with the heavenly world. So, in this modern age, it is important to be alone and take even a short amount of time to read books. The content of the book, or what to read, is also very important.

Having said this, the world has now become busier and noisier with the increase in the number of books and the volume of information. So, you may often find it difficult to find a quiet moment to read a book in the way I just described.

Some people find it difficult to study at home, so they go to a coffee shop, for example, to read *The Six Codes* [the main body of law of Japan] on their laptops when studying for the bar exam. I have also experienced studying in a coffee shop, so I understand the feeling. They probably study in a place where there are many people, including those who smoke, because they cannot focus at home. Perhaps they intentionally choose such a place because what they are working on is so difficult that they want to drop it after studying it for an hour. These people can probably work without being distracted even when there is some background noise.

Regardless of the kind of place you choose, there is a need to make time for silence in your life. Nowadays, there is even music to set a tranquil atmosphere, so making use of such music every now and then may also help deepen your state of mind.

A dangerous state for religious practitioners

In modern times, even religious practitioners live in an environment in which various miscellaneous events rush toward them, so they too may find it very difficult to find a quiet time. When I was single, I used to live in a rental apartment, and although I feel bad for saying this, I was often bothered by package deliveries. For someone practicing religion, there is something unbearable about the sudden ringing of the doorbell. At the time, the delivery person would arrive unexpectedly at any point during the day, so it was quite bothersome for me. I am thankful to have someone else receive my deliveries for me now.

The ringing of the doorbell or phone is truly troublesome while one is in the middle of reading, writing, meditating, or communicating spiritually. I was especially annoyed when the phone would ring while I conversed with a spirit.

The phones nowadays are quieter and also have email, so things have become better, but the phones back then had a jarring sound and were bad for the heart and head. I truly do not like telephones. When I was working in a trading house, I would receive 100 or even 150 calls a day. The calls kept coming in regardless of my situation, so it was really troublesome.

As a religious practitioner undergoing religious discipline or teaching people how to concentrate one's mind, if you become unable to take notice of these things, you are in an extremely dangerous situation. You are in true danger if you are unable to sense that the incoming of information and other interruptions are hindering your work and contemplation. Please be deeply aware that this is an extremely dangerous state for those in religion. These are the main points of this lecture.

Aiming to deepen your religious life day by day

Especially in youth, you must handle tasks that would normally be regarded as painful, unpleasant, or bothering at times. However, even such tasks can be carried out in an alpha-wave state rather than a beta-wave state once you have surpassed a certain threshold and become able to do them easily, as if time had stopped. For example, if you move about in a busy and hectic way, like in a restaurant during lunchtime, you will naturally be in the beta-wave state. But this would not necessarily be the case if you work quietly in a smooth flow.

In this sense, there will always be spiritual training you must undergo as a normal human being, and there will always be spiritual training left for you even when you get old. In fact, corruption may start to set in as soon as you think your spiritual training has been completed, so you must be careful. Please also note that it is also important to diligently carry out even monotonous tasks day after day because they will help you maintain your rhythm of life and prevent you from losing sight of the purpose of your work.

As the material civilization or machine civilization advances, many inventions and new devices will be created, and companies will constantly push you to buy them. But some of these devices will not necessarily benefit you spiritually, so please be mindful of what you use and what you discard from the possible options. When it comes to reading, it is essential to select carefully the materials that will benefit you intellectually or contribute to your work. I hope you will understand the importance of saving yourself from the flood of information and making a wise choice.

Avoid being totally cut off from society

As we live in an age of excessive information, selecting, blocking, or discarding certain information is also essential.

However, if that becomes your main focus, you could become weak at worldly matters, so you must make sure not to go to an extreme.

At Happy Science, we often hold spiritual conversations, and there was a period in the past when we were mostly shut away from the world in divisions like Religious Affairs, the core part of the religion. But as people were trained in such an environment for too long and "holy silence" was overly practiced, many ended up becoming unable to handle worldly matters. They would make mistakes in carrying out worldly tasks, giving rise to problems at a later time.

There was no problem when issues were concealed and the staff was doing their work quietly. But when issues grew serious and blew up all at once, they would come report to me and surprise me greatly. It was like a frightening trick at the end of a haunted house tour. I would immediately return to "this world," and would have to make a decision based on the knowledge, discernment, and decision-making skills I had gained during my days working in a company. There would be times when I even had to recall the legal knowledge I had learned as a student. It would indeed be a frightening experience.

So, when it comes to worldly affairs, it is important to deal with them smoothly and have them done swiftly without leaving them unresolved. Please make sure to have a good balance between spiritual and worldly matters.

As you move up in status, you may want to advance in a direction in which you can maintain a pure and clear state of mind. But please know that there will always be worldly tasks for you to do and there will never be a time when you are no longer in need of any spiritual training. Even in things of this world that you perceive to be trifling at first glance, there may be aspects that shine, like a diamond or gold dust. I hope you do not neglect making an effort to skillfully extract such brilliance.

What determines your work in 10 years

This lecture was a little different from my usual talk; it was, in a sense, about the modern Zen life, or how to make use of Zen in the modern era and incorporate and apply it in modern religion. Many of the points I described here are probably obvious to people who have undergone spiritual training at Happy Science for many years, but I imagine many young people have forgotten about these things. There are several important points, so do not dismiss them by saying that the times have simply changed; instead, study them once again and always keep them in mind.

In addition to the topics of religious discipline and Buddhist training, Happy Science also covers other teachings, such as "enlightenment of management" and "political insight." When such topics are involved, we could become entangled in worldly work and the bustle of secular life. Even at such times, I believe we must have an unshakable self at the core.

There are times when your work is hindered by someone's *ikiryo* or an evil spirit of a deceased person, but by regaining the habit of carrying out the basics, you can block out these influences and keep them at a distance. It will also help you create a "spiritual screen" to ward off these beings. Please do not forget this.

Life is built up one day at a time, so settle all matters that happen each day without carrying them over to the next day, and lead a smooth life. In doing so, I hope you will feel the development of your religious character and the deepening of your religious life.

I continue to study even at this age because I believe that what I study now will determine whether I will be able to keep working in 10 years' time. I believe what you study at 50 will determine whether you can still work at 60, and what you study at 60 will determine whether you can continue working at 70. This will most probably continue to the end of one's life. At around the age I am now, many friends and old acquaintances are nearing or are already at the end of their working careers. But if you hold your aspiration high and continue making efforts, I am sure a new career path will keep opening up for you. Please keep this in mind as well. This concludes my lecture of a religious nature.

CHAPTER TWO

Q&A SESSION ON
"THE POWER OF BASICS"

Q&A session given on September 4, 2016
at Special Lecture Hall, Happy Science, Japan

Q1

The Secret of Keeping to

"the Power of Basics" over One's Lifetime

Welcoming basic questions

RYUHO OKAWA

Looking at the contents of my lecture "The Power of Basics and the Time of Silence" [Chapter One], I feel I need to take some questions. If you have any basic, simple questions, I would be happy to answer them.

It does not have to be a high-level question. Even if some matters are obvious to those who have undergone religious discipline for a long time, they can seem confusing to those who have yet to deepen their studies or religious life. So, please do not hesitate to ask.

QUESTIONER A

I thank you deeply for this precious opportunity today. As I carry out my sacred duty, I have had the opportunity to witness your hard work. Seeing your efforts, I have keenly felt your infinite love for us disciples and the people of the world in your dedication to the finest detail. I am deeply impressed simply by being witness to such efforts.

I would be grateful if you could share with us your secret to how you can constantly make efforts day after day in keeping with the power of basics, while discarding yourself and wishing for the happiness of many with an endlessly pure heart.

My experience of developing a critical eye at about 20 years old

RYUHO OKAWA

I am thankful that you see things in such a positive way. In general, even highly successful people in society can appear like Mt. Fuji, which seems impressive from afar, but has piles of garbage and plenty of useless junk when seen up close. It is commonly said that Mt. Fuji is littered with empty cans and garbage when climbing it in the summertime, and is not a sight you want to see. So, I am secretly fearful of the people who work close to me. They have many opportunities to see me when I am relaxing or off guard and may tell others about me, saying, "Did you know...?" Even though this is something I fear quite a bit, I do not really hide anything.

Now, I am not sure if this answers your question, but I myself have changed as I have aged. Unlike how I am today, I considered myself to be rather clever when I was younger and began to develop a critical eye toward other people, particularly during my late teens and early 20s. There was a time when I saw myself as a wise person, but I was quick to notice the shortcomings of others. It was during a period when I was studying very hard and trying to cram in as much knowledge as I could; it was also a time when I was developing my abilities rapidly.

Such a time can be likened to trying to climb a mountain with all your effort, but since I was "climbing the mountain" so fast, as if I were riding an aerial lift, I began to see everyone else as though they were far below me; many of their faults, flaws, and shortcomings, like their lack of study, stood out to me. Honestly speaking, there was such a period for me.

This was how I was, especially in my late teens and early 20s. When I talked with others, I could roughly tell what books they had read within the last week. During conversations, I quickly understood which books their opinions were based on. It was insolent in a way, but I could often figure out what kind of books they had read and what books they were basing their opinions on. I could easily detect it when people borrowed ideas and opinions from a certain book written by a certain author and tried to make them look like their own.

Similarly, when attending classes taught by professors 20 to 30 years older than me, I would often identify the weaknesses of their research, flaws in their theories, or the incompleteness of their interpretations, rather than being convinced and accepting their lectures straightforwardly. I would listen to their presentations rather critically, spotting the missing points. This is how I was when I was young.

However, things gradually changed after I started work, and I was often scolded for various things. I was told that before criticizing other people I should realize that I myself was unable to complete even small tasks. Such small tasks were really of a simple nature—things that were considered basic. In other words, I often failed to do things that most people should be able to do naturally and was reprimanded for them. For example, I would forget things, be careless, forget to do something someone had asked me to do, forget to take notes of important matters, lose the notes, or mix my work life with my personal life. All sorts of problems surfaced because I had not fully mastered the "basics."

So, I was frequently scolded with comments like, "Instead of criticizing others, you need to see that you can't do the basic things everyone else can do. Aren't you aware of that?" I had rather depressing experiences like this. Of course, I soon recovered even if I had been put down, but in any case, receiving this kind of criticism made me realize that I needed to take another look at myself.

Whether you are "altruistic" or "selfish" greatly changes around age 30

I continued to study even after I started working. Since everyone at a company is required to be useful and productive while working together in a public space, it took a tremendous amount of effort to make time for myself in a life where I would always be tired and busy day after day.

Those who have struggled to squeeze in time for themselves and are able to continue doing so are often perceived to be egoistic, unsociable, or self-centered; they may sometimes be criticized for it. However, looking not only at my life but also at the lives of others from a long-term perspective, there are some surprisingly common traits in people who succeed in making "sacred time" or a "time of silence" for themselves in their busy schedules and continuing to do what they believe they should do or to study what they believe they should study.

One of the traits is that, although they may appear quite selfish, self-centered, or egoistic at first, as they continue to concentrate on improving themselves for a certain amount of time, they eventually start to show the opposite quality. In other words, the efforts they have put in for themselves start to become altruistic endeavors. Oddly enough, although they were making effort to find time and continuing to study for themselves, after a certain point, they unknowingly develop a sense of mission to do something that will benefit others, make people happy in some way, or produce something that will help others. This holds true not just for me, but also for other people who are trying their best to do so. People who may seem to be taking time for themselves in a selfish manner at first glance actually tend to become altruistic later on.

On the other hand, when people are young or are in positions where others have authority over them, some have a difficult time saying "no" to attending social events involving their friends, colleagues, or superiors, and get carried along by the people around them who insist that they be sociable. They end up being taken to various events and allow their time to disappear by letting others consume it. These people may appear to be selfless, sociable, and good-hearted people at first glance, but after a certain time they will find that their "stock" of knowledge has run out.

If used well, the skills and know-how of getting along with others can certainly be a tool to get on well with superiors; to a certain degree, these can help people network with coworkers, make connections to get ahead, or get promoted at work. Some people may appear to have succeeded in becoming popular by allowing others to have authority over them and using their time to get along with others. However, since they have not continued to study to improve themselves and do not have anything to produce on their own, they tend to start taking from others after a certain age. I have seen many people like this in the past.

Since they do not have much to offer, they end up relying on others to teach them many things, guide them, and give them instructions. In this way, their position becomes reversed. I have seen many such cases—those who initially appeared selfless wind up living selfishly by taking love, whereas those who appeared to live selfishly at first gradually become altruistic. This tends to happen around the age of 30. It seems to me that a major change occurs around this time.

In this sense, an evaluation of someone in their 20s does not become permanent so easily, nor should it at that age. Their potential is not fully known yet, and in some cases, it can be different from how it appears on the surface. So, we should not judge people too quickly. Since there are various degrees of importance in work and in relationships, there may be times when you simply cannot decline a social invitation or work obligation. But if there is something you feel you should do no matter what, it is natural that you strive to make time for it. It is also a question of whether there is actually something you want to do.

With regard to your question, looking back on my life, I probably appeared rather egoistic when I was young; there were times when I thought myself to be clever while I looked down on other people and passed judgment on them. I was rude enough to even criticize my supervisors or superiors when I discovered their flaws. In a nutshell, I may have had something like a "sense of chivalry" in that I would side with the weak while going against the strong. I had a slight tendency to attack anyone with higher authority and protect the weak, but this seems to have changed at some point.

Various changes in the process of becoming a public figure

After that, I went on to found Happy Science at around 30, and began giving lectures in front of audiences and writing books as a religious leader. Frankly speaking, when I first set out as a religious leader at 30, I felt as if the "gears" in my head were turning at an incredible speed [*laughs*]. Even though there were many people older than me in the audience, I felt like I could answer any question. At that age, I was full of confidence and felt I could answer any question that was asked.

However, as I continued to work and succeeded in making our organization bigger, I gradually began to feel a certain sense of "fear." It was not because I had failed in any way; the work itself expanded and we were doing well. As the organization grew, people of various social backgrounds, specialists with deep knowledge, and members of all age groups started to join in great numbers; they would listen intently to what I had to say. These people did not exactly voice their opinions, but as the group of people attending the lectures became more diverse, I began to feel a deep sense of fear sinking in. When I watched recordings of my lectures and the answers I gave during the question-and-answer sessions, I would increasingly feel embarrassed, and it would make me want to hide somewhere. I felt very strongly that I needed to study more in order to continue with my work.

Moreover, as I became more well known, the media, particularly the weekly magazines, began to criticize me personally. In a sense, this is part of the process of becoming a public figure. But since I still did not have sufficient experience at the time, I was shocked and upset to see my name appear in various critical articles. I could not believe what was printed. Since there were hardly any handbooks that gave instructions on going from a private individual to a public figure, I had to learn from personal experience, which was rather difficult to do.

To rephrase this from an opposing perspective, only when you see others writing critically about you can you use those criticisms as a "mirror" to look at yourself afresh. The criticisms do not just insult or demean you, but are actually cleverly pointing out your weaknesses; they may be showing you that you are speaking without understanding your powers objectively, even though you are already in a position of leadership and have great influence over others. They are not just rude comments, but are sharp pointers that pierce through things you should be aware of but are not.

You may very well get upset and be hurt by such criticisms, but after thinking about them, you will notice that you are simply lagging behind in your growth and development. If you are used to receiving such criticisms, you could respond tactfully to those comments or manage to change yourself in response. There would be different actions for you to take.

At the age of 30, I was full of confidence and felt like I could answer any question, but I did not receive much criticism because there was only a limited group of people listening to my lectures and reading my books. But as the range of the audience gradually widened and reached a point where my messages were being spread to a national or even international audience, criticisms from various ranks and angles I had never expected started being directed at me. I was surprised by the different views people had.

Feeling the need to become a "professional" of religion in the early 1990s

I think there were some mass media organizations that ambitiously tried to drag me down in the early days of our organization. Around 1990, there was an editor-in-chief of a magazine who had graduated from the University of Tokyo's Department of Religious Studies three or four years ahead of me. At the time, there were many young scholars who were active in the field of religious studies. Some of those who were of the same age group as the editor-in-chief wanted to hold a roundtable discussion by "inviting Ryuho Okawa, surrounding him with 10 religious studies specialists from the University of Tokyo, and interrogating him."

I cannot recall the name of the magazine, but they intended to harass me in public by bombarding me with technical questions; they thought that even though I had graduated from the same university as they, I was from the Faculty of Law and did not study religion seriously. In a sense, they were reacting to and protesting the fact that someone with a law degree had trespassed into their field of expertise. So, I was "invited to participate" in such an event that was intended to publicly humiliate me. However, I did not accept the offer since I was busy at the time.

I also read various comments about me in other publications and found that the criticisms were coming from experts and scholars who specialized in religious studies or Buddhist studies. Since I wanted to spread my teachings widely, I tried my best to use common words to make my messages easier to understand. This would make them available to the general public and people who are not journalistically inclined. But the people with backgrounds in religion, philosophy, or Buddhism apparently felt that I did not know the technical terms well enough. These were the kinds of criticisms I often received.

Then, the "Friday Incident"* occurred. We tried to settle the incident on our own and solved it over time, but it also caused me to reflect on myself. I realized that as long as I worked in religion, I must be professional. Until then, I had worked based on materials I had read within the range of my

---

* TF: In May 1991, the weekly magazine *Friday* (published by Kodansha Ltd.) and other publications started to write many malicious, fabricated articles slandering Happy Science, trampling on many people's faiths. Happy Science members reacted to the accusations and carried out demonstrations and other protest activities.

interests or the subjects I had learned in school or in society, but these were not enough; I had to be professional to be accepted by other experts in the field. So, in the fall of 1991, I started to change my attitude.

We took the case to court and made various legal maneuvers, but they were all legal battles. Fighting the mass media by filing a lawsuit would be how a person with a legal background would fight. So, as we carried out such activities, I also decided that I had to be able to fight in a different, more religious way as well. This was when I had a change of heart and decided to begin studying anew.

Criticisms from the mass media that led me to reflect on myself

During the 1980s, there was a Japanese photo magazine, published by Shinchosha, which sold over a million to about 1.5 million copies a year in its heyday. Around the time when the publication reached a turning point, they secretly snapped pictures of me as I was leaving my home in Nerima ward in Tokyo, where I lived at the time. There was a period when several critical articles were written about me.

Because of that, I moved to a location that was not known to the media, where I resided for several months. This was when I felt I should start studying afresh. I thought, "They may be doing this out of jealousy, but perhaps they condemn me because they think I am not worthy of the success I have achieved." In the eyes of the world, it probably appeared like I had not invested enough in myself and the basics, and still lacked study to gain the level of success I had attained; becoming famous in spite of that may have been unacceptable to them.

After graduating from the Faculty of Law, I went on to study commerce and international trade at a trading company, but since then, I have been writing religious books regarding people's spiritual minds and ways of life. By 1989 and 1990, I had already become listed as a high-income taxpayer in a certain income category. Although I was not classified into the "writer" category, my books were known to "sell well" in general.

At the time, the Japanese government used to issue a ranking of high-income earners. I would have been at the top of the "writer" category, but since I was also doing other activities, such as giving lectures, I was classified in the "other" category, which included individuals involved in cultural activities. Even in that category, I usually ranked around third. The top was usually Ikuo Hirayama, the former President of Tokyo University of the Arts, and in second place was either the head of Urasenke [a school of Japanese tea ceremony] or the lyricist for the singing group AKB48, and I was often competing for third place.

In short, those who criticized me saw my success as "suspicious" since I had not "invested myself" in basic studies as a religious leader. People with degrees in religion who worked in scholarly jobs or as magazine editors started criticizing me first, followed by other people of various backgrounds. Even though I graduated with a law degree, I was young and still lacked insight into law and politics, so those in the political journalism field pointed out where they thought I was "talking big."

Thus, as the range of our activities expanded, people started criticizing me as if to say, "We will not allow you to succeed so easily." That was the impression I got. In 1991, I think well over 50 articles were written in a critical tone by various media organizations, but there were also points for me to self-reflect on as well.

An event that made me realize becoming a professional is not easy

Around fall of that year, I started studying books on religion, including a big, thousand-page, encyclopedia-like book called *The Dictionary of Religion*. I read them from cover to cover because I was determined to make sure there was not a single thing I did not know. I would place this big dictionary on my living room table and start reading it with the resolve to learn all the terminology relating to Buddhism and other religions.

I also read technical textbooks on Buddhism, and around 1992, after about a year of study, I began publishing books on Buddhist teachings. Happy Science believers probably felt that my teachings had suddenly become difficult, with many technical terms.

Before this, there were criticisms from some of our believers as well. There were actually two Dai-sojo monks [the highest level in the Buddhist priesthood] of Tendai Buddhism among our members, and after reading our monthly magazines and other materials, they would comment critically that I had not studied Buddhism enough whenever they visited our local branches.

However, after I started putting out a number of books specialized in Buddhist teachings, they quickly became silent. I received a report saying that they stopped criticizing me because they understood how well-read I was. They apparently commented that they previously thought that I did not understand Buddhism well, but had come to see that I was in fact explaining things in a way that was easy to understand in a modern context. I realized that once I changed myself, the people around me soon changed as well. I also felt deeply that it was not easy to become a professional.

If I was too easy on myself, the people around me who managed the organization would also become easy on themselves. In such circumstances, we can neither understand the criticisms of others nor see what we are lacking. This kind of situation continued for quite a while, causing various problems within the management and in the relations with others outside our organization. In order to get your work done perfectly, you must be a professional and have a far greater level of skill and knowledge than the average person.

On a separate occasion, right after giving a lecture at Yokohama Arena, I published a book, *Kofuku eno Hoho* [lit. "The Way to Happiness," published by IRH Press], which included that lecture. In that book, I explained some of the simple teachings of Happy Science in very easy terms so they could easily be read by many people. I took this approach because I wanted everyone to know the Truth, but some criticized it, saying that it was too easy a way to compile a book.

The determination to continuously develop an organization

When you work, there will naturally be some visible achievements that stick out like the tip of an iceberg, but there must also be a "store under the surface"; otherwise, you lack stability as a professional. To lead a religious organization for a long period of time, one's effort is far from sufficient without such store.

Much like a successful author or critic, I had also studied enough to be able to make a living for myself and support my family. I knew I had enough writing ability to accomplish these goals, but leading an organization over a long period without faltering is far more difficult than the work of a normal author. It is not enough to write a book on my own and have it sell. For example, Professor Shoichi Watanabe, whom I respect and wanted to be like in my student days, probably felt satisfied with being able to support his family and buy necessary books with the royalties from his books.

On the other hand, there are about 2,000 staff members at Happy Science. Back in 1991, we already had over 1,300 staff working for our organization. Of course, not all staff members are single; many have families. In order for these people to be able to continue work throughout their lives, it is not enough just to provide them with "food, shelter, and clothing." We must also have a store of what would be the equivalent of weaponry and ammunition for the military; unless we have enough "weaponry and ammunition"—or enough "work content"—we will be unable to continue our work and activities.

In the early days of our organization, all our staff members took tremendous risks to work at Happy Science. There were unfortunately one or two times when we had to ask a number of them to return to secular life due to poor management. We managed to get through such difficult times because the then chairperson, who was much older than me, worked very strictly and kept a tight hold on matters. Even so, there was much for me to reflect on.

To create something, many things are required. For example, you need raw ingredients to make bread. If you run a bakery, it is not enough to simply make bread for one day; you have to keep your business going. You cannot be content with the level of work necessary to bake and sell bread well for one day at a festival. Moreover, if you employ staff, you have to protect their jobs as well. Recalling my youth from this perspective, I cannot help but feel how small I was when I was puffed up with pride in my 20s and when I thought I could answer any question in my 30s; I was satisfied too easily.

In the past, Happy Science was frequently described as a young organization with a young founder in his 30s. In interviews with people from outside our organization, many commented that I was young. But before I knew it, I am now over 60. With 2,000 staff members, Happy Science is currently expanding its mission into new fields, such as education, politics, and overseas activities. We must now focus on how to maintain and further develop these activities.

In essence, the leader at the top is like a "guarantor" for the assets, education, finance, and sustainability of the business. So, leaders need to be prepared to do everything by themselves if anything goes wrong. When thinking about this, we still have many insufficient areas to improve on. We are still far from the level where we can say we have finished studying; at this level, we cannot say we have done enough no matter how much we accomplish, nor can we say that we know enough regardless of how much we know.

Realizing the lack in the power of organization

You need to be a "professional" to some extent at the work you do now. This is a matter of course. Besides your current work, there will also be other tasks you have not yet dealt with or even talked about that will likely come into your sphere of work in the future. You need to study such subjects in advance and be prepared for the next stage.

People sometimes ask me why I am humble, but it is not that I am humble; I keenly feel that I have not done enough. Despite not having done enough, I will eventually have to face the difficulties that come with age, no matter how hard I try. This happens to everyone, and I am no exception. Looking at the many people in the world whose work performance declines with age, it will not be so easy to defy this pattern. I know that it will be difficult even to maintain the status quo unless I put extra effort into training myself physically and mentally for work and for other situations. So naturally, I cannot help but automatically become strict with myself.

While I have become stricter with myself, I have also begun to feel more like praising and helping people with potential to grow—those who are still unable to display their ability or achieve their goals due to lack of training. In this way, I have developed the exact opposite state of mind from when I was young.

In any case, I still believe I have not done enough at all. I started out by doing everything myself, but now that decades have passed and the organization has gradually taken shape, it may seem like we are operating smoothly to someone looking from the outside. In reality, however, there are still many areas in which work is done based on my intuitions, much like in a company where the founder still works.

In order to maintain our organization as a going concern, or as a "sustainable enterprise," we must create the "genes" that enable us to make progress while constantly changing ourselves. There is still much room for us to improve in accomplishing greater work with the help of other people. I always feel that certain improvements must be made in this regard.

Take, for example, the recent American superhero movies that have been popular. While it is possible to make a movie like *The Avengers*, where a team of superheroes fights together to battle a common enemy, what if a much greater evil were to attack? The Avengers do fight aliens, but if an army of aliens attacked Earth in reality, it would not be possible to fight back with just a team of a few individuals; the enemy would be too powerful. To defend Earth, we must organize a global team to fight together systematically; otherwise, we could never win.

In the same way, Happy Science aims to achieve large-scale work on the global level. However, although the work that was done individually is now being shared with the people around us, we have yet to gain the power of organization necessary to carry out the satisfactory level of work in the eyes of the general public. I also feel strongly that we have yet to amass the power of many people to gain greater strength and increase our influence as an organization. We are still lacking in these efforts. These are my thoughts regarding our overall situation.

Striving to set aside time for something important

I certainly want everyone to work hard. But how much more work one can do is a yardstick to measure whether one's organization still has room to develop. Just as I said in the lecture previously [Chapter One], I always remind myself that what I study now will affect whether or not I can keep working 10 years from now.

The majority of people in my age group are nearing the end of doing significant work, and there are probably not many who are studying for work they will do in 10 years' time. If they were asked, "How about studying for the work you will do in 20 years?" the number of those who are making efforts would be even lower. But when I consider whether I can continue working in 10, 20, or 30 years' time, I strongly feel that I should study what will be needed in the future, even if it may not be useful now.

My answer to your question has broadened into a wide range of topics and become a little long, so you may find it difficult to understand. But if I were to limit my answer to young people, here is my suggestion. Young people can spend much of their time studying if they want to, or do some other activities like working part-time jobs or volunteering. As a religion, Happy Science also needs students to volunteer at our local branches, and I cannot keep them from doing such activities. Even so, I believe they must strive to set aside time for something important in their busy schedules.

Among the books I read when I first started working at a company was a book called *How to Live on 24 Hours a Day* by Arnold Bennett.[*] He wrote about how to spend the 24 hours you have in a day and suggested to look carefully at your own 24-hour day, and somehow strive to set aside an hour and a half—that is to say, 90 minutes—within a day. You can probably set aside more time on the weekends, but the crucial point is whether you can create this time on weekdays without depending on your days off to do so. He essentially says to make 90 minutes of time for yourself at all costs; try securing 90 minutes of your day no matter how tired you are from work or how busy you are, and be careful not to waste those 90 minutes. This is one way of thinking.

If you are a full-time worker who often has to do overtime or keep social obligations with work-related people, you will probably have to give up on many things to regularly find 90 minutes for yourself every evening. For example, you may have to forgo several social engagements with coworkers

---

[*] Arnold Bennett (1867–1931) was a British novelist, playwright, and critic.

and only participate occasionally, or you may have to turn off the television if the programs you want to watch are not really beneficial to you. You may also have to consider whether the overtime work you bring home is truly worth doing. Furthermore, instead of taking your work home, you may have to change your work pattern by thinking about tomorrow's tasks ahead of time and adopting a "preparatory" style.

Unfinished work takes up the most time

After pondering Bennett's message—use 90 minutes for something important—I thought that one example would be time used to read classic books. However, it is not so easy to make such time because businesspeople usually come home tired at night. According to Bennett's observation, those who work in the city of London all read newspapers on their morning commutes. As soon as they arrive at the station, they rush through the ticketing gates and arrive at their offices with weary brains to do the day's work.

Nevertheless, taking a cue from the "90 minute" idea, I strove to secure a slightly longer period of time. To find enough time to read something like the classics every day, it is necessary to create a situation where you have mostly completed your work. This is indispensable.

In my experience, I would use most of my time struggling to complete unfinished work as another new task would come up. When you have unresolved work and are concentrating on getting it done, another task may arise, and as you are overwhelmed by the additional workload, yet a third matter may come up. When unresolved tasks pile up in this way, efficient time usage becomes extremely poor. You could then become completely stuck and preoccupied with the thought that "Maybe I have to spend a week, or even a month, to get all this done."

Even after you have gone home, you may not be able to stop thinking about the unfinished work, and often find yourself unable to focus on other matters and feel extremely exhausted. I have also experienced this, and I think most people have. At such times, you may perhaps feel like relieving your stress and relaxing by going to a beer garden to have a drink with your coworkers and later to a karaoke bar to sing. It may feel like you have gotten rid of the stress, but even if the stress from that day is gone, you will have another depressing workday the next day. In most cases, you will end up repeating this kind of cycle.

So, if you want to make time for yourself, it is vital to think about how to get your work done during business hours. In truth, the heart of the problem lies in how you work.

Quick decision-making and a preparatory style of work

The approach I took to solve this problem was to make decisions as quickly as possible; in principle, I tried to resolve all solvable issues immediately as they occurred. Of course, there are sometimes lengthy issues that you simply cannot resolve right away. In this case, there is nothing you can do but to write a note and post it somewhere to remind yourself of the problem and how you plan to deal with it. There are always tasks that cannot be completed right away.

But there are also tasks you can take care of immediately. It is important *not* to put off a decision you can make today, the work you can complete today, and the response you can give today. By acting quickly on matters you can decide on or provide answers to within that day, you will not leave any tasks pending. This will allow you to respond immediately to the next task that comes up. You can then put all your energy into getting the new task done. In this way, it is essential to tackle each task one by one, and get each one done completely. In other words, you need to create a situation in which you have no tasks remaining at the end of the day so that you have plenty of time to spend on work the next day. Then you will be able to make time for yourself at night and even study difficult subjects.

As you make progress in your work, you can do more than just act quickly to deal with any issues that come up. In my case, I often went to work early before regular business hours, and the first thing I did was to list all the tasks I anticipated would come up that day and determine how much time I would need to complete them. I would think of how to use and allocate my time to get each task done and work in a preparatory manner to have certain materials ready. In this way, the materials would be available as soon as anyone needed them. This is how I used my time. This approach will allow you to complete your tasks ahead of time, and you will begin to have more free time.

Since I worked in this way, no matter which department I was transferred to, people working there ended up having more free time. Even in departments that had a reputation for working late—until 9 or 10 o'clock, or into the night—once I was transferred there, all work would often be completed before lunchtime. People would say to me, "How strange! Our workload is disappearing. The tasks all vanish as if being sucked up with a vacuum cleaner."

Whenever I completed my own tasks and freed up my time, I would offer to do more tasks as well. Others would take me up on my offer, entrusting me with piles of work they had struggled to complete. I would simply tell them, "OK, I'll take care of it," and clear away all the work as if it were being sucked into a vacuum cleaner. With these tasks disappearing quickly, my mind would always remain calm. I experienced such a phenomenon.

Normally, the amount of work to be done varies depending on the day, and businesspeople in Japan are often busier at the end of the month or on days that are multiples of 5 or 10. However, some female coworkers would tell me that I always seemed to have a lot of free time, and that I consistently cleared away my work smoothly even when others were panicking to handle the wave of work that suddenly came in. I was grateful to hear such comments.

So, when you are young, you need to be strict with yourself. You also have to make your own personal time and use it as "time to study for the future." To do this, how you get your work done is essential, and you must try to keep in mind that "Today is my whole life." This is an important attitude to have.

I had a greater ability to "compress" work

My work at the time often involved negotiating or having discussions with people. Usually, talking to people inside the company is easy, but negotiating with people outside the company is quite challenging. In my case, I mostly dealt with bankers.

When conducting business in an orthodox Japanese style, it generally takes at least three separate meetings before finally reaching a conclusion. Prime Minister Abe[*] met with President Putin many times, but this is the typical Japanese style of negotiation. People usually get to know each other in

---

[*] TF: At the time of the lecture.

the first meeting, form a slightly closer relationship and hint at their intentions in the second, and finally indicate what they want to negotiate toward the end of the third meeting.

Japanese people dislike discussing issues at the first meeting, but I would usually talk in a friendly manner, go into detail as much as possible, and continue discussing until we reached a conclusion to close the negotiation in just one meeting. I would often adopt this style of negotiation. While others visited the banks three times, I usually closed deals in just one.

There are conflicts of interest between different business organizations, and business is often a zero-sum game. In other words, when one side gains profit, the other side loses, and vice versa. In such a business relationship, people are competing for a "fixed pie." Based on this approach, one side winning the negotiation means the other side loses, but in my case, the other party usually ended up becoming a fan of me after our short conversation. Since I spoke in such a way that pleased them, they would eventually start to think seriously from my perspective.

Even when the calculations clearly showed that the bank would lose money if they accepted the conditions I presented, they would end up yielding, saying they would make up for the loss by negotiating more severely with other companies. As our negotiations proceeded, they would change their attitudes in this way. Given that I founded a religious group later, maybe it was a form of "mind control" [*laughs*].

There was a Japanese TV drama where the main character said, "It's a deal!" whenever a contract was settled. [Note: The TV drama *Your Home is My Business!* aired from July to September of 2016 in Japan, starring Keiko Kitagawa.] While this is not exactly the same, I would save time by using a technique to conclude a deal in one negotiation. There were times when my potential adversary ended up siding with me. I remember these kinds of mysterious phenomena happening often. Since I adopted such a method at work, I probably had a greater ability to "compress" my work compared to other people.

So, although I was swollen with pride and was strict with others when I was young, as I aged, I gradually became stricter with myself while being less strict with others. This sums up my background information to answer your question.

Q2

Using High Technology Wisely

QUESTIONER B

Thank you very much for this precious opportunity today. My question is on how to live in a modern material civilization, which you mentioned in the main lecture [Chapter One].

In modern society, there is an increasing number of opportunities for us to use computers and the Internet at work, and people involved in technology development and engineering probably work mainly with "things." As a result, I'm afraid they tend to become overly enthusiastic about modern gadgets and forget about human emotions, or neglect religious activities, because they are always preoccupied with objects.

Please tell us the secret of how to prevent ourselves from being carried away with high-tech products in such circumstances.

The positive aspect of smartphones

RYUHO OKAWA

I am not particularly well versed in modern technology, and since there are many companies that contribute to our economy by producing material objects, I should choose my words carefully so as not to make them suffer an economic downturn. While various devices are being sold on the market as products of "convenience," there are actually two sides to these devices: one side that truly provides convenience and another side that consumes your time. So, we must be careful.

I certainly find smartphones to be convenient at times. Nowadays, everyone can use one, and people can find things that formerly would have been looked up in an encyclopedia.

Back in the day, encyclopedias only served to decorate a father's study or to be part of the background in a drawing room. People would purchase them for hundreds of thousands or a million yen [thousands or ten thousand US dollars] but hardly read them, except for doing a little research when they were first purchased. Encyclopedias are quite heavy, so when you try to look up a topic and realize that you are searching in the wrong volume, it is quite bothersome to have to bring out another volume.

When encyclopedias were used at home, they were mostly used to look up medically related topics, such as a certain disease that a doctor mentioned in a diagnosis.

There were encyclopedias at my home when I was a child. My father was admitted to a hospital in Tokushima City for about 40 days during my freshman year in university, and when the doctor told us that he had a stomach ulcer, my father was worried that it was stomach cancer. When I went to visit him in the hospital, he told me, "Go home and look up stomach cancer and stomach ulcer in the encyclopedia. Then, bring me a copy of each of their descriptions because I need to find out if the doctor is correct." So, I wrote down the differences between the symptoms of stomach cancer and a stomach ulcer. I do not think photocopiers were available at the time, and I remember copying down the main points by hand and bringing the notes to him as I was told. In the end, it turned out to be a stomach ulcer, but my father had feared that it could be something worse and thought stomach cancer was a possibility.

This was probably the extent to which encyclopedias were used. Since I could not carry them out of my house, the only way to make the information accessible was to make copies of certain pages to take with me. In this way, people used encyclopedias to occasionally look up things, but since the topics of interest would often be found in different volumes, portability was a problem. In this sense, smartphones are quite useful to look up all sorts of information.

The dangerous aspects of smartphones

Nevertheless, smartphones are insufficient sources of information for people whose occupation involves writing books or speaking in public. It has certainly become much more convenient to casually look up different kinds of information on smartphones than in encyclopedias, but to write books, you need to read materials in book form on the related subjects. Otherwise, your work would be inadequate by professional standards and end up being like one of those essays written by college students which all describe the same ideas.

Some university professors ban students from using their smartphones when writing essays because they get frustrated reading so many papers that are based on the same smartphone search results. Smartphones are certainly convenient, but they do not generate any added value in terms of demonstrating individuality or uniqueness, or in making you stand out among others. So, although smartphones are useful to obtain information quickly, those aiming to become professional writers need to be cautious not to rely too much on them.

Furthermore, I feel uneasy when I see people crossing the street while fidgeting with their smartphones. I also read in the news that the first death in Japan involving the smartphone game Pokémon GO was confirmed in Tokushima Prefecture. It seems that the person was playing Pokémon GO while driving, so it is not surprising that an accident occurred.

In this way, if you become too absorbed in using your smartphone, you could lose yourself and end up in some kind of failure. Although I admit that smartphones can be convenient, you should think carefully about whether it is really for you and use it wisely. Sometimes people need smartphones for work or their hobbies, so it is worth noting that you do not need to use them in the same way as other people.

Focusing on what to create, rather than on environmental conditions

At the end of 1989, Happy Science moved into the Kioicho Building, a location with one of the highest rental rates in Japan, but since we did not have much to do and it was quite spacious, we ended up hiring many people. I decided to rent an entire floor in the building because of a book I had read about Honda Motor Co. It described how the company's internal communications improved significantly after setting up an office with enough space to accommodate the different divisions, where people from different divisions could gather and hold meetings more easily. Following Honda's model, we chose a building that had a big open-floor layout. The floor space was about 1,250 square meters [13,500 square feet], so it was large enough to accommodate all our divisions.

When we first moved in, we only had 200 staff members, and much of the floor remained unfilled. For this reason, we continued to hire people for about a year. People of different work backgrounds were hired, and whenever new staff joined, new desks and chairs were set up for them. Such office furniture alone was not enough, so phones were installed and everyone was given a word processor. Seeing word processors on everyone's desks, I wondered what kind of work they would be doing, but even they did not know. They assumed everyone would need a desk, chair, phone, and word processor, so those items were purchased.

The Happy Science chairperson at the time would have to sell off those desks and chairs whenever some changes occurred, like when we moved to a different location or downsized our workforce. We were not a used goods retailer, but there was always something being sold off. The organization had the tendency to buy things even when we could have leased them. Since administrators did not know how to use such a large space, they developed the habit of filling the empty space by purchasing desks and chairs and seating themselves there.

In 1996, too, when our general headquarters was moved into the Head Temple Shoshinkan in Utsunomiya City in Tochigi Prefecture, they filled the large space with staff desks. This is the first course of action everyone takes in the beginning. Even when I told them to fill it with people from the outside and not with current staff, they seemed to have difficulty understanding what I was saying and stuck to a simplistic way of placing their desks in the new space. But it is important to think carefully about whether certain things are truly necessary.

On the other hand, some American computer-related companies that develop software have adopted workspaces in which employees are not assigned to a desk, but are instead allowed to work freely on flextime at a long oval-shaped desk shared with other employees. They believe productivity will decrease if they work in too formal a setting. Some even put their sleeping bags on the floor and slept in the office. I once read a book describing such workplaces.

In fact, focusing too much on the "environmental conditions" is a problem. After all, what is essential is "what is created," rather than the surrounding conditions. But people tend to be enthusiastic about preparing the "environment to create something," rather than about "what they create."

Focusing on raising revenue rather than spending it

Happy Science currently operates on a system which constantly increases revenue, but it was very difficult to reach this point because almost everyone in the organization was only enthusiastic about spending money and not about generating revenue. Newly hired staff members who came from other companies generally thought about using the money and would immediately ask, "What is the budget?"

Large companies generally have an annual budget, which is allocated to each division, and people spend it on different purposes, including personnel and transportation expenses.

That is why the newly hired staff would ask me about the budget, but I replied that they would be the ones who needed to create the budget. I told them, "Bring in revenue on your own, and then decide on what and how much you can spend. At this stage, the budget will not simply fall to you from above," but they would have a very difficult time understanding what I was saying because they had never worked in an organization that had no budget.

This is certainly understandable. In a small company, those in managerial positions have a grip on the flow of money, but once the company gets bigger, it is harder for them to keep track. Even if they do not know whether the funds were borrowed or earned, the budgets are allotted to each headquarters, then to the departments, and to the sections. A section chief then thinks of ways to control the expenses within the allocated sectional annual budget. If the budget is tight, he or she may consider cutting staff from 20 to 18 people, asking section members to reduce transportation expenses, or limiting the section's total entertainment expenses to a lower amount.

But Happy Science was still in the development stage in those times—budgets could only be made if there was revenue from some kind of work, and different divisions were handling incomings and outgoings separately. The division responsible for raising revenue was very optimistic when reporting prospective revenue. For example, when they heard that a believer decided to donate ¥100 million [about US$1 million], they reported to the Secretariat Division, which instantly included that amount in the revenue account.

The current El Cantare-Belief Promotion Division was once called the Activities Promotion Division, and the people in that division used to say that having enthusiastic momentum was important in the activities, so they had to promote activities with vigor. So, whenever they heard the believers' wish to find new members or donate a certain amount of money, they would immediately take those intentions as "already achieved." The Secretariat Division would then include those figures in the revenue calculations and consider them as money "available for spending." In this way, they planned how to spend before the actual revenue was raised.

In a similar manner, once they decided to create one million new believers, they would immediately begin preparing for the increased membership by buying powerful computers to hold all data on the new believers. They even went so far as to rent more office space to house those computers and to have the floors carpeted to protect the computers from dust. A large corporation with large amounts of funds may do that, but we would often experience failures like this in our early stages of development.

Do not be controlled by machines

After all, machines themselves do not generate any profit. People can generate profit only if they use machines skillfully to produce added value. In the beginning, however, people become "used" by the machines, and end up spending all day on a computer or spending time maintaining, purchasing, or selling these technological gadgets.

I am well aware of what things were like in Japan in the 1960s when computers first started becoming popular. Around that time, the banks started to computerize and other companies followed their lead; people called it "the great revolution." The introduction of computers was expected to reduce personnel expenses. Computer companies were promoting sales, claiming that companies did not need to hire new people because the computers would do the calculations for them in an instant. Banks mostly involved calculation work, but in those days, abacuses and simple calculators were still being used. So when the banks learned that computers could do all those calculations for them, they all started installing them.

However, once they bought the computers, they realized that none of their employees knew how to use those computers and had to hire a lot of computer operators, resulting in even more employees. Their initial plan was to reduce the number of employees, but since their current employees could not use computers, they had no choice but to bring in computer operators. As a result, all the major banks ended up having over 10,000 employees. This kind of strange phenomenon was happening everywhere.

So, while some machines are necessary, you need to carefully consider whether they are truly needed and how they will contribute or generate added value. Of course, it is good to use new devices that are useful, but please be careful not to be controlled by them.

Examples of two company presidents and their uses of technology

I can think of two contrasting cases regarding this topic. The first is about Mr. Konosuke Matsushita. According to his books on management, Matsushita Electric Industrial Co. [now Panasonic Corporation] had been using a POS [point of sale] system to calculate the total sales of each store on a daily basis.

Every day, he would receive a chart with the sales records of every store organized into different categories, showing how much sales each store generated. It seems like he checked the charts for the first month or so, but he soon found them unnecessary. He noted, "Looking at such charts doesn't provide any benefit. I just need to see a report once a month or so to understand the overall results. I want to know whether the sales have increased, stayed the same, or decreased, and which stores are doing well and which are not. There is no need for all this data. I don't need this information anymore," and he eventually stopped using them.

The other case involves Mr. Toshifumi Suzuki, Chairman and CEO of Seven & i Holdings, who resigned in 2016. He used to work at the publication distributor TOHAN Corporation before joining the Ito-Yokado supermarket chain, and he later launched 7-Eleven Japan. While working at Ito-Yokado, Mr. Suzuki was assigned to research the 7-Eleven convenience stores in the United States in the 1970s. At that time, being assigned to such a job was apparently considered to be a demotion. But when he traveled across the United States, he found that convenience stores were very popular and was convinced that Japan would also see an "age of convenience stores." When he introduced the store chain to Japan, not only did it actually become bigger than the 7-Eleven parent company in the United States, but it also became even bigger than its Japanese parent company, Ito-Yokado.

Mr. Masatoshi Ito, the founder of Ito-Yokado and Mr. Suzuki's boss in the company hierarchy, had a hands-on approach and encouraged employees to make firsthand, on-site observations. He said, "Visit the stores of competitors to thoroughly research what kind of products they have, what products are selling, and what new products they have lined up." However, Mr. Suzuki, who was in charge of the 7-Eleven project, kept his staff from observing their competitors. He said that even though there were many other convenience stores entering the market, it was best not to look at their product lineup because it would be tempting to imitate them.

Mr. Suzuki also took a hands-on approach at first and often went to inspect stores himself, but he eventually stopped making on-site visits and started assessing matters through data alone. He studied what was selling from the data collected from all stores, and hypothesized how sales were affected by various factors, such as the weather forecast.

For example, he hypothesized that *oden* [a type of Japanese hot pot] would sell even in June if the weather were cool, and he found that it actually did sell well. Similarly, he refuted the idea that ice cream would not sell in winter, stating, "That is not true. If *kotatsu* [a table with a built-in heater] becomes popular, I'm sure ice cream will sell well." He also claimed that even Christmas cakes with chilled toppings would sell on December 24 if heaters were being used in homes. In this way, he analyzed people's change in behavior through data.

Mr. Suzuki took a contrary approach to Mr. Matsushita; he probably had an aptitude for this kind of method. He formerly had a career at TOHAN Corporation, and after joining Ito-Yokado, he only worked in the general affairs and human resources divisions without having any experience in sales. Because of this, he was considered to be poor at sales-related work, but he actually succeeded in expanding the business by developing business ideas based on data and acting on them. There are cases like this.

However, it would be difficult to fully copy his methods. It might be that he did not reveal all his secrets, so we may not know the whole story of his success; he might have secretly visited the stores of competitors on his days off. Even if he did not go to those stores, he apparently participated in new product taste testing within the company with other executives when a new product was to be launched, so he must have valued his own senses from firsthand experience.

In this way, some people are capable of using results derived from computer data, while others see such data as unnecessary. Choosing which approach to take probably depends on each person's way of thinking.

As a side note, after Matsushita Electric Industrial Co. changed its corporate name to Panasonic Corporation, it became less profitable and adopted the American style of management. Since the American management style emphasizes quarterly settlements, good results must be achieved in a short span of time. The president who decided to introduce the American style managed to achieve a V-shaped recovery by separating loss-making divisions from the profitable ones, but this resulted in the loss of research and development staff, causing the business to decline later on.

Sony Corporation was also once known for its research and development. But when a foreign CEO took office, he cut many loss-making operations, most likely in an effort to achieve results in the short term. Consequently, the company lost the ability to develop products on a long-term basis and fell behind in technological development. Now, the business remains sluggish.

There are different ways of thinking; just like using tactics and strategies in waging war, one's way of doing business should vary depending on where one opens one's shops and who the competitors are. So, one needs to be flexible and free of any preconceived ideas.

Religions must value "high touch" over "high tech"

Machines are now making further advancement, but concerning the prospects of religion as a whole, I sense that a great restructuring could take place if we get carried away by the wave of overwhelming technology. If that happens, many temples and other religious facilities will start to disappear.

An increasing number of Christian churches are already being sold off in the United States. Since church administrations think it is wasteful for a single-story church to take up prime real estate, some churches have been replaced with multi-story buildings, and the church facilities have been moved into the basement of the new buildings. In this way, they could gain income from renting the upper levels to support themselves, regardless of the fluctuating donations from the congregations. Such things happen.

Similarly, in Japan, Hongan-ji Temple, which did not own any land in Tokyo, took a similar approach in opening a temple there. I heard that the only way for them to expand into the capital was to construct a building with rooms and facilities to lease to tenants or businesses, and limit their temple space to just one floor.

I understand that the circumstances have been changing, but to counter high tech, we must value "high touch" and emphasize the importance of heart-to-heart communication and human interaction. Unless we take precautions, there is a danger of religion dying out completely.

In connection to the consumption tax hike, the newspaper companies in Japan earnestly insisted that home delivery services were indispensable. But what would happen if they stopped delivering newspapers and completely changed their distribution style so that newspapers were only available in vending machines on the streets? Newspaper circulation would definitely plunge to levels of "near extinction." That would most probably be the consequence. Most of the time, people will choose to get information from TV, cell phones, or other means, so newspaper publishers are another industry at risk. Managerial decision-making can sometimes lead to the destruction of one's business, so one needs to think carefully when making a decision.

Think about whether a machine or a device is necessary for you

In my case, if I think I can get by without using something, I generally do not use it.

When traveling, there are various modes of transportation available, such as airplanes, bullet trains, local trains, or highway buses, but you cannot say which one is good and which one is bad. The cost of transportation for each method also varies. Some people work on a very tight schedule and have no time to spare. For example, you may have to attend a meeting in Osaka and return to Tokyo on the same day. In that case, you probably have to take an airplane or bullet train. But a student who does not have a job and has plenty of free time may not mind traveling on an overnight bus. This is a matter of choice.

Thus, there is no need to completely agree with others in the use of a particular machine or device just because it is advanced. Instead, you should classify things based on whether they are necessary for you.

Multitasking as a way to increase the amount of time you have

It is important to eliminate what you consider a waste of time, but when something is unavoidable, the only choice would be to make a little more effort to do multiple tasks simultaneously. Looking at people who use their time wisely, I get the impression that many of them can view matters from multiple perspectives and devise efficient ways to work. This may more or less be an innate quality, but much of this ability can be developed through effort.

For example, babies are generally born one at a time, but occasionally there are mothers who have twins. Raising twins is very difficult, because two newborns do not behave in the same way. Since they act independently, the mother must constantly watch the two simultaneously. Even if she complains that she can only take care of one child at a time, she cannot change the fact that two babies were born; she has to take care of both children. It would be a different situation if she were to give one up for adoption, but if she decides to raise them both, she must look after them on her own even while her husband is at work. Taking care of twin boys would still be relatively simple, but raising a twin boy and girl would involve more complications because she would need to buy different things for each child.

When you have twins, you must inevitably be able to multitask; you have to be aware of what the two babies are doing while you are doing some other chore. This is an ability you can develop to some extent through practice.

While baby strollers have been available for a long time, I now see childcare workers at urban nurseries and kindergartens using ones that can carry four to six toddlers at a time. They put the children in the stroller, push it to the park, and let them play there. They seem to be using such baby strollers as a method of transportation. This is one way of saving time.

Although things have become busier in the modern day, time itself cannot be increased. But one way to increase the time you have is to work on multiple things simultaneously. This may seem impossible, but if you think about it, you will see it can actually be done.

Of course, not everyone can do this normally. It is said that the male brain can only do one thing at a time, and the ability to do one thing for a long time is a defining quality of the male brain. But this is not always true. For example, many fathers in Japan probably use their breakfast time efficiently by reading the newspaper and watching the TV news at the same time; they eat breakfast while browsing the newspaper with the televised news playing in the background. They have no time to read the newspaper after breakfast because eating already takes up much of their time. They would have to get up much earlier if they wanted to do so. That is why they do several things simultaneously.

How do they actually do it? They are most likely skimming the newspaper to quickly pick up the important points, and looking at the article headlines and just reading the ones they are interested in. When an important news item appears on television, they focus their attention on it during the feature, but read or eat otherwise.

I once read a story about the international economist Keitaro Hasegawa having an overnight guest. Apparently, Mr. Hasegawa had the habit of reading books while he ate, and when he dined with his guest, he followed his regular routine, which shocked his guest. He read while he ate even in the presence of the guest because that was what he was used to do. This shows how hard it is to break a habit. I am not sure if such behavior is considered polite or rude; it may depend on your position. Mr. Hasegawa wrote that he was surprised to see the startled expression of his guest when he was simply behaving as he always did.

You need to give certain things up when multitasking

I am probably a similar type of person. I often feel short of time, so I constantly think about how to create more time. Nevertheless, it is necessary to spend time on certain things every day.

One example is the time for exercise. When I have extra time, I exercise by going out for a walk. But there are times when I do not have enough time or when the weather is too hot in the summer to go outside. In such instances, I have to think of a different way to exercise.

Another example is when I study English. Since I occasionally give lectures in English as part of my work, I have to study English seriously, so I listen to speeches by foreigners or the English news even when I take a bath. This is one form of multitasking, but even so, I listen to them quite seriously. I also study German and French, but I have yet to surpass the introductory level to be of practical use. I am still far from being able to lecture and write books in those languages. So for now, I have decided that gradually accumulating knowledge over time is good enough. Even so, my German is actually slightly better than my French.

At my request, my secretary records two 25-minute television language programs on German and French conversations every week. To tell the truth, I do not have enough time to spend just on them alone. So, while viewing one of the German language programs, I also do some exercises. For example, I do high knees while jogging in place or throw some boxing punches. Sometimes I do sit-ups while listening to French. In these ways, I combine exercising and language learning together.

In some ways, I multitask knowing that I am giving up on certain things; I am aware that I will not remember everything even if I were to focus all my attention on those language programs. Unlike a student, I do not have as much time to watch those programs or to read textbooks repeatedly. I am certainly grateful to my secretary for recording the programs, but since I only watch the 25-minute programs once, it is unlikely that I will remember everything.

So, I consider it a positive result if I can remember some of the content even slightly. It does not matter whether I am jogging, doing sit-ups, throwing punches, strengthening my chest muscles with a training tube, treading on a bamboo stepper, or doing anything else at the time. A certain amount of information will enter through my ears and eyes, so it will not be totally fruitless; there will be some benefit. Even if I do not remember 100 percent of the material, I can still retain maybe 10, 30, or 50 percent of it.

If I continued this for a year, there would be a few more things I could understand. After two years, the scope of my understanding would expand even more. This is generally how I think and what I practice.

Fragmented language study can become connected at some point

There are times when I sleep soundly at night, but on many occasions, I wake up in the middle of the night due to various concerns I have. If I cannot go back to sleep, I usually read foreign language textbooks, so that I do not waste time simply lying in bed and worrying about things. I do not read English books, but instead read textbooks on other languages. Since these materials are moderately difficult, I soon become drowsy and cannot read them for long. They have such kind of effect, and that is the important point.

If I read an English book, I might end up reading it until dawn without realizing it, so I choose materials I cannot focus on for too long. The best material would be something that would make me sleepy after reading it for about 10 or 15 minutes. Materials that are somewhat challenging and difficult to understand are just right. In this way, I have the habit of reading such textbooks whenever I wake up in the middle of the night; it is like taking a sleeping pill.

Even though I read these textbooks as a substitute for sleeping pills, some of what I read remains in my memory. It may be better to read the textbooks while watching the German or French conversation television programs, but since I exercise while watching those programs, I cannot refer to them. So instead, I read them little by little when I wake up in the middle of the night and watch the programs during the day while I exercise. I split the content I study in this way in hopes that all the information will eventually blend together inside my head.

In any case, that is how I create time. I adopt a multitasking approach, discard what I find unnecessary, and give up on things to a certain extent without seeking perfection.

For example, I listen to English in the bathroom, but I cannot always catch 100 percent of what is being said, especially when I am taking a shower. What is more, our bath is designed to circulate heated water 24 hours a day, perhaps to make it easier to keep the bathtub clean. It is a rather high-quality model, with hot water cascading like a waterfall from a wooden spout made from Japanese cypress, and it circulates the water continuously. This is probably to filter the water and remove any dirt or impurities to make it easier to clean, but since it makes an extremely loud sound, I cannot hear the entire recording of the English CD.

If I turn up the volume too loud, the sound would bother my third son studying on the floor below. He often complains that the sound of the English CD was too loud last night or that he was woken up by the sound of English in the morning. So even though I usually try to listen at a volume I can hear clearly, I sometimes have to turn it down. I lower the volume when it is late at night or early in the morning, but if I notice that my son is awake, I listen to it at a higher volume.

Even so, I am unable to hear all the English because it gets muffled by the sound of the cascading water and the shower, but there are also parts that I can catch. And as I listen to the CD again and again each time I bathe, different parts of the English CD come through over the noise on different days. For example, even if there are parts I could not hear because of the sound of the water one day, I would hear that portion another day. By piecing together the fragments of what I have heard, I eventually begin to understand the whole picture and understand the main points. This may seem like a crude way of learning things, but this is how I usually carry out my study.

Make sure not to waste your time
by using electronic devices

To sum up, in regard to the use of technological products, you have a choice of using them or not using them; you can even use them in a different way from how others use them. It is particularly important to learn to multitask at work, so you need to be careful not to become too absorbed in electronic devices when you use one; refrain from spending too much time doing what is essentially unnecessary.

When desktop computers first started being used widely, I was still working at a company. As they became increasingly popular, people at the company had the urge to find uses for them because it would be wasteful to have them just sitting and taking up space. They thought they had to keep them turned on all day to get as much use out of them as possible, so they started to add more work making spreadsheets.

Bosses started to ask their subordinates to input figures to make charts every day, which was totally pointless work. No matter how many charts you make, it does not contribute to increasing profits at all, so it was no different from a hobby and a way to eat up time. Superiors were actually demanding that their subordinates make charts and submit them, simply because they believed it was wasteful not to use the computers. They even made it their work to read those charts, but I felt that all that effort was useless. It is essential to really see whether something is truly beneficial.

Having said this, I cannot speak much about how best to use such devices. I am a "primitive man," and still have the lifestyle of "the primitive age." Buddha lived during the ancient Jomon period of Japan, but maybe I am also of the "Jomon period." Different kinds of technology are now part of my life to a certain extent, but I limit my usage to an absolute minimum. Maybe "someone of the new age" could invent a clever way to use these devices. I cannot be bothered by such things, so I am just waiting for something better and more developed to become available.

I am guessing you [the questioner] usually listen to English language CDs at double speed. I am sure you do. You probably listen to my lectures at double speed as well [*audience laughs*]. You may think it is more efficient to listen to a two-hour lecture in one hour, or a one-hour lecture in 30 minutes, and try to preserve your study time in this way. Those with good listening comprehension skills can listen to English at double speed, so it is possible to make efforts in many different ways.

AFTERWORD

Although many books on Zen are being published even today, most of them are focused on the Chinese classics and their interpretations. Bound by formalities, they end up being discussions for the sake of discussion. As a result, people fail to understand what Zen life is or what enlightenment is.

This book encourages people to lead a modern Zen life using two key phrases—the "power of basics" and the "time of silence." Given that Buddhist enlightenment also includes the pursuit of wisdom, you may feel the spirit of Zen being revived in the modern age, like a spring of clear water.

This book also explains how to increase your ability to do work and describes the essence of an intellectual life. I believe it is a starting point to which people today should once return.

Ryuho Okawa
Master and CEO of Happy Science Group
September 9, 2016

PART TWO

The Power of Basics

and

the Road to Success

PREFACE

This book is a continuation of *The Power of Basics and the Time of Silence*, a lecture I gave while being guided by inspiration. I mainly talked about the religious feeling that flows through everyday life and work.

Secular life and religious life are generally considered to be clearly separated, but I dare to teach the road to enlightenment suitable for people of modern times.

People tend to think that renouncing the world to undergo religious discipline means being secluded in the mountains for a decade or so without any access to newspapers or television and becoming completely detached from the secular world.

To use some expressions from the movie *Chihayafuru*, the religious life I teach is based on the understanding that *araburu* and *chihayafuru* are different; although both tops are spinning at full speed, the crown of the first top sways wildly while the crown of the second top spins upright as if it were completely still. Those who go far are always calm in mind.

Ryuho Okawa
Master and CEO of Happy Science Group
June 3, 2017

CHAPTER ONE

A LECTURE ON
"THE POWER OF BASICS"

Lecture given on October 8, 2016
at Special Lecture Hall, Happy Science, Japan

1

An Important Power to Win in Life

Building one's basic strength

In September of 2016, I published the book *The Power of Basics and the Time of Silence* [compiled as Part One of this book]. Despite its unusual title, it was favorably received by readers. It seemed like there was a greater need for a book on these topics than I had expected. So, I decided to give another lecture on the same subject to provide supplementary material.

The reason for doing this is because the power of basics is extremely important for religious life and discipline. People have a tendency to look only at the final results—these are usually the only things they see—but what is actually vital are the efforts leading up to these results. Such efforts serve to build one's basic strength.

For instance, you may be charged thousands or tens of thousands of yen [tens or hundreds of US dollars] for a portrait drawn in five minutes by someone who has been an artist for decades. You may complain that it is too expensive for such a quick drawing. But if the artist explains, "It may have taken only five minutes to draw this, but it took me 30 years of practice to be able to do it," then you may no longer object. It is clear how big of a difference there is between what an average person can draw in five minutes and what a professional artist can do in the same amount of time.

In the case of religious leaders, since they must basically be experts in the studies of life and human beings, they must not only have different kinds of knowledge but also a store of experiences. They need to be more observant than the average person to study the various types of relationships, the fluctuations of life, and the successes and failures of people. They need to look at different kinds of lives: those who manage to recover from failure, those who cannot restore their livelihoods, those who give up because they are discouraged, and those who fade away despite experiencing success. Religious leaders must observe people's real lives and also study them through novels, movies, and TV dramas. In this way, I do not consider life to be so easy.

Hidden efforts made by top-level people

In particular, those who aspire to be number one in the nation or in the world need to be aware that there is a truly long way to go to achieve such a title. They need to know that they must not become easily satisfied with themselves.

In the summer of 2016, the Olympics and the Paralympics were held in Rio de Janeiro. Everyone was probably only interested in the results of the games and did not know much about the practice and training that each athlete went through in the four years leading up to the big event, or perhaps for an even longer period of time. The efforts of some athletes may have been known to some extent, but those of most athletes remained unrecognized. People judge athletes based on the performances they see in a short competition without knowing all the efforts that lie beneath the surface.

However, we must realize that everyone makes a "hidden effort." So, one cannot simply envy the gold medalists without having put in the same amount of effort as them.

The same is true with top-level actors and actresses; there is something different about those who are repeatedly offered the leading roles in TV series or movies. For the viewer, it might be exciting to see different actors and actresses in each show, but in reality, we tend to see the same faces again and again. This may give the impression that the producers are cutting corners by using the same performers everyone is familiar with for the different roles. Nevertheless, the competition behind the scenes is quite fierce; those who rise to the top to play the leading roles have managed to survive a strict screening process.

When people make a debut, they first draw attention by winning a contest where only one is chosen from 5,000 to 10,000 candidates and come on the scene in this way. Then they actually sing or act in more performances to get evaluated. They may succeed in the first performance, but fail in their second, and be tested in the third. As they repeat such experiences, they are gradually weeded out. Even if two people have equally good looks, one will remain unselected and disappear while the other will survive and repeatedly get roles in TV series or movies, allowing that person to continue to widen his or her range of acting capabilities.

The necessary attitude for building unwavering status

A similar tendency can also be observed in the business or work environment. As new shops open one after another and old ones go under, the selection process continues to take place repeatedly. Such replacement of the old with the new may be a trifling matter for outsiders, but it would be a great issue for those who are in the middle of the competition.

I went to New York to give a lecture several days ago, and in my talk, I mentioned that the number of Starbucks stores in New York vastly increased compared to the last time I was there eight years earlier. [Note: The lecture, "Freedom, Justice, and Happiness," was given in Manhattan, New York, on October 2, 2016.]* I remember there were a lot more hamburger restaurants in the past, so I imagine that market competition has been fierce within the small area of Manhattan. There must be real competition over better services, as well as a "soft war" going on regarding the taste of

---

* TF: The lecture is compiled as Chapter Two of *The Trump Secret: Seeing Through the Past, Present, and Future of the New American President* (New York: IRH Press, 2017).

the food and other elements. Even though people in general do not really know what is going on in the background, there must be a significant difference between the shops that manage to survive and those that do not.

Coffee shops and hamburger restaurants are often thought to be the kinds of businesses that anyone could run after a certain amount of training, but even these shops are subject to selection. There is such an indescribable harshness in business. Even among franchises of the same brand, some stores go under while others survive and improve their performance. This is probably due to the creativity and ingenuity of the shop owners, as well as their natural character.

The power of basics is the effort an ordinary person makes to improve things day and night for 5, 10, 20, or 30 long years, while being fully aware of his or her mediocrity. As you continue such efforts, you will gradually build greater strength and capabilities. I believe this is one of the attitudes necessary to achieve an unwavering status where you are highly recognized in society.

The importance of humility in achieving ultimate victory

There is naturally a disparity in people's talents. Many people may feel this way, and this cannot be helped. Particularly in the case of young people, since there is not much difference in their life experiences, many may just look at their short-term achievements and feel the gap in talent between themselves and others.

So, I am not saying that there are not any differences in people's talents. There certainly are. However, no one can actually tell from the outset exactly how much difference there is in people's talents in the truest sense. Ultimately, people are mostly judged in hindsight and regarded as having talent based on the results.

It is certainly better to have talent than none at all, and it is fortunate if such a talent is recognized by others. But if your efforts and results fail to meet others' expectations, you cannot be successful. You must know this.

At Happy Science, we conduct "past-life readings" and often reveal that a person was previously born as a well-known figure or had achieved greatness in a past life. On hearing this, many people may take interest in that person and decide to attend his or her lectures. However, as they listen to more of that person's lectures, some of the audience may feel like they are wasting time and money and gradually stop attending. As a result, there will not be many people who will come and listen to his or her talk.

The reason for this may be that the speaker has been lacking in his or her efforts and discipline in this lifetime, despite having high potential. So, the person must humbly accept the objective results that currently appear before him or her. The person needs to humbly reflect on the result he or she now faces and renew his or her resolve to make continuous efforts.

The word "humility" is often used lightly, but humility is important not just because it is a moral virtue. It is not a mere social skill to get along with other people. It is certainly true that people find it hard to criticize or speak harsh words to humble people. Rather, humble people often receive praise from others, so being humble could be regarded as a way of getting through life. However, only those who truly recognize their own weaknesses and diligently keep up efforts to fill in what is lacking can be the final victors.

After all, winning in life does not mean winning against other people. You must win against yourself before winning against other people. You cannot just expect good results to come without having won against yourself.

What is more, even if you manage to win against yourself, there will also be many who have risen above others after having won the fight against themselves. The victors and losers will be determined yet again as a result of the competition with these people.

People may say that there was a difference in the level of talent by looking at the overall results. Or if they do not see any difference in talent, they may see a difference in luck. In any case, you must accept the end results.

The traits of those who succeed and those who fail

Rohan Koda[*] wrote in his *Doryoku-ron* [lit. "Effort Theory"] that people can be divided into two categories: One type attributes their success to their own greatness and blames other people, the surroundings, or other factors when they fail; the other type puts more emphasis on gratitude and thinks, for example, "I owe my success to the people around me; they helped me to succeed," "I was blessed with a favorable environment," or "I am successful because I was given a chance."

Of course, there might be many reasons for failure; it could be that it was someone else's fault, your parents or siblings' fault, a bad environment, the government, or financial problems. There are probably many people who will justify their failure with such excuses until the end of their lives. However, Koda stated that he had never seen anyone who held such a tendency achieve success.

In times of failure, it is important to take the blame in its entirety and reflect on the possible reasons it happened, including insufficient effort on your part, weakness in your way of thinking, or your lack of virtue, and then redo your work. It is important to think of things based on the Law of Cause and Effect.

---

[*] Rohan Koda (1867–1947) was an idealist Japanese writer who contributed to the development of modern Japanese literature. His works include *The Five-Storied Pagoda*, *Encounter with a Skull*, and *The Bearded Samurai*.

People who take responsibility for their failures and acknowledge their own lack of effort in the process will often find that a path gradually opens up to them, and they will eventually succeed. On the other hand, prosperity and success will not last long for people who tend to think, "My current success is due to my talents and abilities," or "I am lucky because God loves me." While luck is certainly something you can draw toward yourself, it is a mistake to excessively attribute your success to your self-centered efforts. Rather, successful people feel keenly that a lot of support and help they received from others made them what they have become.

People who continually experience failure tend to blame other people or the environment. As a result, they gradually hold a grudge against the world and are pushed out of society. Some people shut themselves away in their homes, while others lead rebellious lives or turn to illegal behavior. Some might even become criminals or inadvertently take another's life. When dissatisfaction toward society becomes excessive, people become unable to forgive the world, and their rebellious feeling toward God can turn into extreme, hurtful acts against others. This can really happen, so we need to carefully consider our tendencies.

2

The Difficulty of Continuously Winning

in a Democratic Society

Even the most distinguished people struggle to keep winning

Even if one has talent, that alone does not guarantee success. This is an undeniable fact in this world. For example, it is said that even authors who have won prestigious Japanese literary awards, like the Akutagawa Prize or the Naoki Prize, are advised by their publishing companies or certain editors that they should not quit their part-time jobs, even if it is a job at a convenience store.

What they mean to say is, "People may think winning such a nationally prestigious award means that the authors have a talent for writing, and they would, therefore, finally be able to make their debuts as professional writers and earn their living from writing, but reality is very harsh. Royalties are calculated based on a price per page, so writing one short story would only be worth about ¥400,000 [about US$4,000], which is not enough to support oneself. But a job as a convenience store clerk in Japan will guarantee you at least ¥2,000,000 [about US$20,000] per year."

It is certainly true that the income you earn while working at a convenience store would be the same as what would be earned from writing five short stories. But in reality, writing five short stories for publication in a magazine is hard; it is not something that can be done easily. If you think about it, you will understand that true talent is not a one-time success. Even if you believe you have talent, it is difficult to have talent that would enable you to keep winning.

Take, for example, Soseki Natsume[*] from Meiji Era Japan [1868–1912]. He was sent to England as the first student chosen by the Ministry of Education to study abroad. After returning from England, he taught English literature as a lecturer at the First Higher School and Tokyo Imperial University. He then quit lecturing to author a serial novel in *The Asahi Shimbun* newspaper. That alone was perceived to be quite a sensational event by society at the time.

Soseki had accumulated the basic skills and knowledge to be able to earn a living as a novelist. At the time, he, along with Ogai Mori,[†] was probably one of the most intellectual figures in Japan. His level of education may have been incomparable, not only within Japan but all of the East. In this sense, he probably accomplished enough learning that he would not run out of ideas to write about.

---

[*] Soseki Natsume (1867–1916) was a prominent Japanese novelist in modern literature who wrote *Kokoro*, *Botchan*, and *I Am a Cat*, among others.

[†] Ogai Mori (1862–1922) was another prominent Japanese novelist of the Meiji period. His works include *The Wild Geese*, *The Dancing Girl* (Maihime), and *The Abe Clan*.

In addition to Japanese literature, he was able to read classical Chinese literature, and he had studied English literature while abroad. So, his accumulation of knowledge was much more than that of other people. Since his base of knowledge was more comprehensive than the average novelist, he probably had plenty of ideas to write about, but even with such talent, he died before turning 50 years old.

According to the written records of his wife, Kyoko, Soseki's friend had sent a telegram to Japan saying that Soseki had experienced a bout of insanity in London. She also mentioned that when they were living in Japan, she had noticed many of his eccentric behaviors, making her wonder if her husband had gone mad. This shows how difficult it is to continuously engage in creative work. Even for Soseki, who had an overwhelming advantage over others in terms of intellectual ability, education, environment, and talent, it was not easy to make a living by writing novels in serial form for a newspaper.

In any case, Soseki often acted eccentrically, to the extent that his wife worried that he had lost his mind. Apparently, he also had a violent temper. We need to understand that creative work can be this harsh.

The same can be said of Yukio Mishima,[*] who displayed a talent for writing from his youth; a novel he had written

---

[*] Yukio Mishima (1925–1970) was a Japanese novelist whose works include *The Sea of Fertility*, *The Temple of the Golden Pavilion*, and *The Sound of Waves*, among many others. A right-wing nationalist, Mishima attempted a coup d'état that ended in failure, which led to his suicide by seppuku.

as a high school student was published in a magazine. Not only had he written novels, but he had also excelled in other studies. After graduating from the University of Tokyo Faculty of Law, he joined Japan's Ministry of Finance. However, he resigned within a year to become a writer. Mishima's intelligence and talent were made evident from a young age.

He probably dreamt of living life like a successful Western writer, who would produce a major piece of writing once every three or four years and spend the rest of his time relaxing, having fun fishing for marlin, going over his thoughts while on the water, fully recharging, and preparing to write his next work. He aimed to attain the kind of life where he could live off the royalties of writing a major piece once every few years. However, even someone with as much talent as Mishima could not make it. In reality, he had to write a novel every year to earn enough to get by. When he wrote his major work, *Kyoko-no-Ie* [lit. "Kyoko's House"], he apparently aimed to live like a famous Western writer and take a few years off to relax, but this dream did not come to pass.

These examples show how hard it really is to keep winning, or to keep surviving, even for a person who is said to be in the top class. It goes without saying that you need to work hard. You also need talent. Even so, you cannot always win or survive. This is reality.

A harsh principle that sustains a democratic society

In a modern democratic society, people are given many opportunities and there are various roads to success. However, in some ways, this is an extremely harsh age compared to when society was based on a class system because we live in a world where society grinds people so that they will not become conceited or corrupt.

A democratic society is based on the premise that people can judge others even on matters that are beyond their own capability. There is such a principle in democracy. For example, even if you have no aptitude for music, cannot write songs or sing like a professional musician, you can still judge whether a professional singer sings well or not after listening to their song. Of course, your judgment may not necessarily be reliable in ranking the work for its excellence, but it is nevertheless the evaluation of one person. It is believed that when enough individual evaluations are collected, the common critiques become obvious. So, even if you cannot create music, you can still judge whether it is good or bad when you listen to it.

The same is true with hotels. Even if you cannot manage a hotel, build one, or provide any services, you can still judge whether or not a hotel has a pleasant atmosphere by staying at one overnight. If a given number of people evaluate a hotel on a scale of one to five, for example, a certain degree of objectivity will be gained and the differences between various hotels will also become clear. This is also true for movies. Nowadays, people freely evaluate movies by ranking them with a number of stars on a scale. The assessments probably differ from person to person, but once a certain number of evaluations have been gathered, people will look at them as an objective judgment of the quality of the work.

A democratic society is based on such a premise. Even in presidential elections, people who are "not as distinguished as the president" vote for the president. This means that people can judge whether a candidate deserves to stand above others and is suitable to be their leader. Unless we accept this, there cannot be a democratic society.

From the perspective of those who cannot become professional writers, someone who can write novels may seem far superior in comparison. Even so, anyone can decide if a novel is interesting or not by reading one. For instance, you may find that the book you bought at Osaka Station and read in less than three hours while riding the bullet train was boring. This may be just one opinion of one reader. But the overall opinion of 100 readers judging whether it was good or bad would be more or less the same as the average opinion of 10,000 readers. In this way, the disparity between writers who sell well and those who do not begins to show. This is a harsh reality, but we must accept it.

I imagine people who appear on television are constantly fighting to gain higher viewer ratings, but the opinions of the general public show a fairly accurate evaluation when pooled together. Sometimes you may feel that the results are not as good as what you expected. This is unfortunate, and it may be due to bad luck or an unfavorable environment. Other people may have been blessed with better conditions. Even so, you should not put blame on those factors alone. I cannot help but feel that this is indeed a harsh reality.

Raw talent alone is not sufficient

The singer Hikaru Utada recently resumed her artistic activities after a hiatus of several years. It appears that she has made a comeback after declaring she would suspend her activities to "concentrate on human activities," during which time she got married and had a child. I listened to the songs on her return album, but they were quite different from her former songs. I remember her old songs as being melancholic and sorrowful.

She made her debut under her own name when she was about 15 years old. At the time, I wondered why she sang in such a melancholic and sorrowful way for someone of such a young age. Then it turned out that she was the daughter of the singer Keiko Fuji, though she had kept it a secret at first. Given that her mother was Keiko Fuji, it is no surprise that she has inherited an exceptional voice. Keiko was blessed with some hit songs in the earlier part of her career, but not in her later years. This probably made her life very difficult. On the other hand, even though Hikaru Utada made her debut without disclosing her relationship to Keiko Fuji, she attracted many fans with her voice, and her songs became huge hits.

She then stepped away from the music industry to get married and have a child until she made her recent comeback. When I listened to her new songs, I found that her melancholic, sorrowful tone had faded. Her songs have become much happier, perhaps because she has been quite satisfied with life. Of course, she has a certain level of ability, so I presume her songs would be equally popular, but she is no longer the same "Hikaru Utada" that she used to be.

I used to wonder how someone aged 15 to a little over 20 could sing in such a sad, melancholic, heart-wrenching way, but it made sense to me after finding out that she was the daughter of Keiko Fuji, who sang melancholic *enka* [traditional-style Japanese ballad]. In this sense, she probably rose to stardom because she was blessed with talent and luck, combined with her hard work. But she has changed since then. I am not sure how things will turn out for her in the future, but things like this can happen.

Since talent for music is largely inherited from one's parents, there is a clear gap between people who are gifted and those who are not. However, there are other factors that could emerge later in life, such as one's way of thinking, the amount of effort one puts in, and how one perceives life, so it is worth noting that one does not necessarily succeed with innate talent alone, like a sudden windfall.

Those who benefit from their parents' influence may certainly stand in advantageous positions, but they may also face difficulties, such as becoming targets of jealousy. Take, for example, the Japanese actress named Anne, who often appears in TV dramas and movies. Her father is a famous actor, but she apparently made her debut without disclosing that information. She probably wanted to test herself to see if she could become popular and be regarded as having talent while keeping that secret. In such circumstances, her abilities have gained recognition to some extent. Of course, she must have secretly put in effort to study acting, including her father's work. Such cases do exist.

Whether in sports, the entertainment business, or academic study, there are many kinds of talent, but raw talent alone will not lead you to success. It is like a rough diamond dug out of the earth in Africa; an uncut diamond does not have sufficient value in its original form. Its value is determined only after it is cut, polished, and attached to some piece of jewelry, like a ring, so there is some amount of effort required. Needless to say, if you do not recognize that the stone is a diamond and it is discarded as a piece of quartz or glass, there would be nothing to become of value.

Ultimately, it is possible to attribute people's success to differences in talent or destiny. For example, it is said that the court musician Salieri suffered from jealousy as a result of the difference in talent between him and Mozart. It cannot be helped if you simply cannot contain your jealous emotions that arise as you pursue your path. But still, you should not complain unless you have done everything you can. Sometimes you may feel like resenting God, but you must do what must be done.

If by chance you are not talented enough to succeed, then you should concentrate on doing what you can do within the scope of your own talent. It is important to know how to be content and live within the scope of your efforts.

3

The Strictness of Being a Professional

The harshness of competition

Competitions in real life are truly intense. Regarding the singers and actors I mentioned earlier, only one or two people are selected from a field of many candidates to become a star, and as competition continues among the select few, some will end up disappearing from the scene. New faces keep appearing one after another, making the competition extremely harsh.

There was a two-part movie called *Chihayafuru*, which came out in Japan in the spring of 2016. I missed both parts when they came out, but I was able to watch them on DVD. The movie turned a competitive *karuta* [Japanese card game] tournament into a teen story. People might usually think of *karuta* as a simple game of picking out *waka* poem cards played during the New Year holidays. But the movie depicted the game as an extracurricular club activity in school, where the members of the competitive *karuta* club began each practice by running to train their bodies.

In fact, physical strength is indispensable to keep playing the game; the players need to train their bodies because competing in a series of games is exhausting and leads to a loss of focus. It seems like their mental ability decreases when their blood sugar levels drop, similar to when studying for exams.

The movie also depicted how the club members would practice their hand movements for a *karuta* competition, just like a baseball player would practice swinging a bat. Since the players need to instantly pick up a card, these hand movement practices are part of their training. I am not sure if this is true or not, but in the movie, the players would flick the cards so quickly that one was flicked into a *fusuma* door [a thick-papered sliding door] and got stuck there. It is unclear how much of the movie was based on the truth; if a card were to be flicked fast enough, it could happen. In their training, I sensed the same kind of intimidating element found in swordsmanship or ninja training.

To play the *karuta* card game, one needs to memorize the Ogura anthology of 100 Japanese *waka* poems, but this alone is not enough to win. You have to develop physical strength, quick reflexes, and the power of mental concentration. You must also continue doing basic training to keep your brain working, maintain willpower, and improve teamwork. These are all very tough things to do, and I thought it was quite a difficult game.

As a side note, Suzu Hirose starred in the movie and made her debut as the lead role. As a teen film, the movie focused on a unique theme. Since the movie was based on a popular manga series, it may have already had a market to appeal to, but normally, a movie about *karuta* would not easily be a box-office hit. It was also well made, and there was something inspiring about it.

In a competitive *karuta* game, the players sit face to face, and when the first half of the poem is recited, the players race to search and identify the matching card that has the second half of the poem written on it. In the movie, the main character [Chihaya Ayase] played by Suzu Hirose had excellent hearing; she had the ability to sense the vibration of the "f" sound before the complete Japanese syllable "fu" was voiced, and would identify the relevant card instantaneously.

Perceiving things before they actually happen

I got the impression that competitive *karuta* is quite similar to the world of Zen meditation, swordsmanship training, or *iaido* [skill of drawing a sword]. In kendo, for example, the players do not move in reaction to their opponents attacking. They wear *men* [mask helmets], which only allow them to see the opponent's eyes through a metal grill, so they cannot clearly see the opponent's facial expressions. For this reason, they observe the movement of the tip of the opponent's *shinai* [kendo stick] and footwork to read where he or she would attack.

So, they do not block or parry the attacks after they have been initiated; they sense the opponent's attack ahead of time by looking at the movement of his or her feet and *shinai*. Those with advanced skills can easily parry all the attacks just by observing the opponent's footwork.

The same could be said in other fields as well. In baseball, it may be the same as being able to read the different kinds of pitches.

Incidentally, I remember hearing the following story regarding a high school baseball game. It was when Fumiya Tsuta was the baseball club coach at Ikeda High School in Tokushima Prefecture, which became a well-known school for baseball. One time, after watching video footage of the opposing pitcher his team would face the next day, Coach Tsuta said in front of the reporters' cameras that "The pitcher releases the ball vertically when he throws a fastball, and releases it at an angle for a curveball."

It was actually a psychological trick, and the opposing pitcher who heard his comment was shocked. He could not believe that his pitches could be distinguished even before they were thrown and was completely seized by nervous fear. The opposing team suffered a crushing defeat in the actual game.

After the game, Coach Tsuta confessed, "Well, what I said about their pitcher was certainly true, but our players wouldn't have been able to hit the ball even if they could distinguish the pitches. Even if they were to swing the bat after identifying the pitch, it would still be too late. So, they wouldn't have been able to hit his pitches." He was quite shrewd [*laughs*].

Even though the batters did not have the ability to hit his pitches, the pitcher was shaken and started to doubt his form. He worried about how he should pitch, since he feared that the opposing batter would be able to determine the kind of ball he would throw by looking at his form. In the end, the batters were able to hit his pitches numerous times, allowing Ikeda High School to win the game.

We know that sometimes people can perceive an opponent's move before it actually happens in various competitive settings or games. So, it is understandable that some people might be able to tell which letter is going to be pronounced by hearing the slightest sound. Maybe this kind of eerie ability exists in every field.

Experiences involving my English

Let me tell you about other incidents from my own experience. When I went to Hawaii years ago, an American talked to me, so I replied in plain English. It was a brief conversation that did not last even 30 seconds, but that was enough time for the person to guess that my English was New York English. The person proceeded to ask me which university I had graduated from and where I had studied abroad. I am sorry if this sounds like I am bragging, but to me, it was frightening to know that 30 seconds was enough to identify my English.

As mentioned earlier, I recently gave a lecture in New York, and something similar happened. It was the first time in four years that I had given a lecture in English outside Japan, so to me, my level of English was not satisfactory and I felt I still needed practice. But the local audience who heard my lecture apparently commented that my English was New York English. I am not sure what part of my speech made them have such an impression, but perhaps it could be said that I generally spoke in a fast, clipped tone.

In short, New York English is similar to the way newspaper articles are written; the main points are presented early because the articles could be shortened due to limited space. Since parts that do not fit in the layout will be cut out, journalists train themselves to write the important points first to ensure that they remain in the printed piece. In general, New York English follows a similar format, with the conclusion mentioned early and concisely, and if time allows, additional explanations would follow. This kind of style is often used.

Since I actually experienced meeting someone who recognized my English just by listening to it for less than 30 seconds, such occurrences may be common. Even though people may not have the same ability as the protagonist in a movie who can tell the syllable "fu" from the vibration of "f" even before the syllable is sounded out, I assume the same kind of skill can be developed in any field. A professional writer or journalist can probably understand the writing ability of someone by having that person write a short article or a one to two-page manuscript, just as a fishmonger can determine the kind of fish by looking at a single scale. In this sense, I feel that the professional world can be quite tough.

The severity of the professional world

The same could be said of food industry. It is said that "professional" foodies who dine out at various eateries and restaurants can quickly tell what ingredients were used in the food. For example, it is said that by eating a dish of *ayu* [sweetfish], a true gourmet can even tell which river the *ayu* was caught by its taste. This kind of expertise is depicted in the Japanese manga, *Oishinbo* ["The Gourmet"].

In the cooking manga *Oishinbo*, which was once popular in Japan, the main characters Shiro Yamaoka and Yuzan Kaibara say things such as, "This *ayu* is from the Hozu River," "This *ayu* is from the Shimanto River," or "You can tell where the fish come from just by eating them because the moss they eat changes the taste of the fish." In the professional world, one can provide enough detail to identify what the fish ate as it grew. This is a very frightening world.

This is more or less true in any professional arena, whether it involves cakes, coffee, English tea, or Japanese tea. Sword appraisers probably have the same kind of ability, and so do archers. The same is true for novelists and religious leaders as well. A simple test of quality would be enough to have a general idea of one's capability. The world is a difficult place, and you must not always expect to be lucky without undergoing enough basic training or mastering the basic moves.

Of course, there may be times when you "accidentally get a hit with a swing of the bat." In the past, I too experienced something similar when I was playing baseball during gym class in school. I was in the outfield with my glove hanging down by my side when the ball came flying toward me, and just as I lifted my glove up, the ball somehow landed in my glove perfectly. My gym class teacher was surprised and said that he had never seen such a fluke. It indeed was a fluke; I just happened to bring up my glove and found that the ball had landed there.

Such a lucky event can happen in life, but it is not a common occurrence. The ball does not just fly into your glove; you usually have to go after it to catch it. And in order to chase and catch it, you need to develop various skills, like the ability to run and jump or hand-eye coordination.

In this sense, it is worth noting that even if a lucky coincidence happens once in a while, you should not get too drunk with such luck. In the majority of cases, people win or lose as a natural consequence.

If you understand this principle, you will see that people who easily say, "I am disheartened"—which we often hear nowadays—are quite easy on themselves. There are some people who study or make an effort for just a short period of time and quickly give up once they fail, but such people are not worthy of claiming that they are disheartened. You could make that kind of remark if you have done all that you can and have devoted yourself fully to carrying out the proper basics but failed nevertheless. Normally, people who have not made such an extensive effort often use that expression as an excuse.

4

The Efforts Required

to Remain among the Top

The importance of both talent and effort

The topic of natural talent reminds me of the movie *The Man Who Knew Infinity*. It tells the story of Srinivasa Ramanujan, a genius mathematician from India—how an accounting clerk from India is invited to the University of Cambridge in England and becomes a Fellow of the Royal Society and a Fellow of Trinity College, Cambridge.

In the movie, Ramanujan talks of his experience of a goddess appearing before him to show him written formulas and equations. His experience is so mystical that these formulas are placed on his tongue or closed eyes. I wish I could have a similar kind of experience [*laughs*]. I am sorry for my lack of guidance to those involved in science and mathematics. Maybe I need to form some association with such a goddess who would leave mathematical equations and physics formulas with me.

Ramanujan was considered to be a genius for understanding mathematics despite not having had a proper education, and yet he was thought to be at the same level as Newton, or even higher, and was invited to England. In his work, he would just present the final formulas without providing proofs, which is an important process in proper mathematical practices. He would intuit the formulas much like the enlightenment of Zen, but would not explain the reasoning that led to the formulas; he said he simply saw them. This was considered problematic.

Something like this can happen in the world of Zen meditation; Eastern enlightenment can be attained in such a way. However, in a Western context of logical and analytical thought and perspectives, this was inadmissible. So, Ramanujan was trained to do proofs, but doing so consumed a vast amount of his time, and his life eventually ended early. Even a genius can experience such difficulty.

There was such a person who understood mathematical formulas even without having been taught. Perhaps this was exactly the same in the case of Mozart, who could hear symphonies of the heavenly world in his head. I presume such kinds of people do exist.

Even so, it would be impossible to exhibit such greatness without polishing one's talent. It would be difficult to achieve great success in mathematics if you do not have the necessary oratory or writing skills to prove your work because otherwise you would fail to gain the recognition of others. Having natural talent is certainly valuable; such talent could be possessed only by one in 100 million people, or one in a billion people, or even with greater odds. But you must not be too proud of it. After all, you must make sufficient effort to explain your work to other people with average capabilities.

The difficulty of maintaining one's job performance while supporting a family

Furthermore, whether or not you have sufficient ability to support a family is another matter. The Japanese critic Shoichi Watanabe once mentioned in a general magazine that there are two kinds of geniuses in the world: One is a genius who stays single all through life, and the other is a genius who marries and has many children. When asked which type of genius is happier, he said it is definitely the latter, or the one who has also managed to raise children.

I would say it is not simply about happiness, but also about a difference in ability as well. Maintaining one's job performance or remaining among the top while supporting a family is a very difficult thing to do. Objectively speaking, once you marry and have a family with children, you will need two or three times the ability to do the same level of work you did while single. That is why you need a certain number of years in training before getting married.

You will not be able to support a family unless you have enough understanding of your current job and have mastered it to the point where you do not have to overexert yourself to work. If you need to devote all your time and energy to your work, or focus all your thought just on work, you have yet to reach a level in which you can support a family.

Perhaps this is the reason why many religious leaders stay single without having a family. There have also been many philosophers since the olden days who remained single. Even philosophical geniuses often stay single. To put it another way, this means that they are not able to write books that sell well enough to support a family, or give lectures that gain popularity. Although they may have elevated philosophical ideas, their ideas are often too difficult for most people to understand or support, so they cannot convert those ideas into income. There are such aspects to philosophy.

Kitaro Nishida[*] was certainly a great man, but the image of him cooking dried sardines on a small charcoal grill shows how poor his life was. I imagine he had a very difficult life, mostly because his written works were beyond the comprehension of the general public. His high-level contemplation may have inevitably made his philosophy difficult, and perhaps it is necessary for such philosophy to exist. Even so, I do feel that he could have trained himself to make it more useful for many more people.

---

[*] Kitaro Nishida (1870–1945) was a leading modern Japanese philosopher. Having graduated from the Tokyo Imperial University in 1894, he taught at the Fourth Higher School in Kanazawa City, Ishikawa Prefecture, and later became a professor at Kyoto Imperial University. He is famous for *An Inquiry into the Good*, among other works.

The extra effort to develop a higher caliber
and perfection as a human being

Attaining a level to become a top-rated expert is difficult and requires many sacrifices. There will be many things you have to give up. You truly have to abandon many things, such as relationships, friendships, or time previously spent on leisure, such as drinking, singing karaoke, or gambling. Even so, it is still difficult to reach the top.

What is more, even if you manage to reach the top, when you try to live in an ordinary way like other people, the various chores of everyday life can often hold you back and prevent you from doing your work. For example, a professional *shogi* [Japanese chess] player may focus on studying *shogi* strategy at home while relying on his wife financially and hoping to eventually earn a living from professional *shogi*. In that situation, if the wife asks the husband to go buy some ingredients for dinner, the time spent shopping would prevent him from focusing on his studies. But such a scenario could arise if he were solely dependent on his wife's income.

There is a well-known Japanese professor at the University of Tokyo whose wife is also a professor at another university. I once read that he has to take out the garbage in the morning at the request of his wife. Even someone like a professor at the University of Tokyo must do his share of the housework if he is married to a career woman. He may be told, "It's your job to make breakfast," "Taking out the trash is your duty," or "Giving the baby a bath is your role." Under such circumstances, he may not be able to demonstrate the same ability at work as when he was single.

Nevertheless, complaining is just an excuse. It simply shows the limit to your talent. If you cannot produce good results because you are asked to do other tasks, are distracted by your family, or have to take care of your children, that is the limit to your ability and that is the extent of your talent. This is something you need to know. If you have limited talent and want to overcome it, you must make extra effort when other people do not. And you must keep doing so. It is necessary to accumulate such effort.

It is possible for one's abilities to decrease after getting married. This holds true for professional wrestlers, professional baseball players, *shogi* players, schoolteachers, university professors, and novelists. It can certainly happen in any field of work; it is true even for employees and business owners. Marriage comes with much miscellaneous work, and if you are not willing to carry out what is required, problems will be sure to occur in the household. You must take care of all these responsibilities; otherwise, you cannot develop a higher caliber or perfection as a human being.

Expanding the scope of your work through task delegation

In addition, you also need to expand the range of work you can do. Incompetent people do not usually feel gratitude when others do things for them, but it is important to know how grateful it is to be able to receive help from others.

When other people help you, their help becomes meaningful only if your work efficiency is increased and greater value is added to your work in proportion to the amount of help you receive. Some form of payment or salary is probably given to those helping you, but for the remuneration to be paid, you must make further progress in your work as a result of their help.

For example, Sadamu Ichikura's[*] books on management state that once a company grows to more than a certain size, even the president of a small to medium-sized company must hire a secretary because this would enable the president to do several hundred times more work. This may sound quite strange and incomprehensible for someone who has never had such an experience.

Many presidents of small to medium-sized companies are actually quite versatile and competent; they can do almost anything and tend to do everything themselves. To begin

---

[*] Sadamu Ichikura (1918–1999) was a leading Japanese management consultant who gave advice to more than 5,000 companies and revived many companies that were on the verge of bankruptcy. He was known to give direct guidance to company owners based on his belief that 99 percent of business success depends on the president.

with, they could not have started a business if they did not have such talent. However, once their companies exceed a certain size, they must learn to delegate tasks to others. More specifically, the presidents should have others do lighter tasks or fixed procedures, while they take on new projects, more challenging tasks, or work of greater value. Unless they shift their work in this way, their companies will not grow.

This is one of the bottlenecks in running a business. The presidents of small to medium-sized companies are generally skilled at many things and quite capable as individuals. But to develop their companies further, they need to delegate tasks to others even if it is something they can do themselves.

Producing more added value upon rising to a higher position

Although a person who is assigned tasks receives a salary for the work being done, it would be pointless if the president cannot work on tasks of greater importance using the time that was created by delegating work. If delegating work simply means giving one's work to others while the total amount of work remains unchanged, the amount of money paid to an employee as salary would be a drain for the business. Unless the same amount is deducted from the president's salary, it would not be possible to maintain a financial balance.

According to Ichikura, hiring just one secretary makes a huge difference. Presidents of small to medium-sized businesses usually handle a variety of tasks, such as managing their schedules, answering telephone calls, meeting with people, running errands, holding interviews, and receiving packages. By hiring just one secretary, they can make these tasks flow quite smoothly.

Nevertheless, he also writes that many people are unable to make use of a secretary efficiently. If people have more important work to do, they can make greater progress by having one person working for them. But for those who cannot recognize the important work they should be doing, hiring a secretary may only be causing losses, a drop in productivity, or an increase in expenses from the perspective of business management. These points need to be understood well.

Happy Science staff members can be promoted to the positions of general manager, director general, executive director, or even higher. Once they obtain these positions, they may assume that they will have many subordinates to manage. But they need to give it serious thought.

When given a greater title, if a person thinks they can relax because they have many subordinates to do the work for them, then that person is definitely not of managerial quality. Despite having attained a higher status, a bigger salary, and a number of subordinates that gradually increases from zero to 5, 10, 20, and finally 100, if a person does not learn to produce work of greater worth that exceeds the help received, then that promotion is unjustifiable; it was a mistake. If someone appointed to a higher position becomes a mediocre staffer who feels happy to be able to relax while the subordinates do all the work, then that promotion was a failure.

The crucial point is this: Having someone help you means that you should produce even more value than before. This is the same as how married people, who once thought it was sufficient to work just enough to support themselves as single people, realize that they need to produce greater results when supporting a family.

5

Ways of Thinking That Enable You to Keep Winning 10 Years from Now

Life is truly harsh. It is important to win in the present, but you also need the wisdom and effort to keep winning 5 to 10 years into the future. It is certainly better to have talent. But not many people can recognize true talent in others from the outset, and those with talent often go unnoticed. Even if you train someone you think has talent, there are numerous cases where these efforts are wasted. This shows the severity of the competitive world. However, competition is necessary to keep people from becoming conceited and corrupt.

In the real workplace, even a ¥100 [about US$1] difference in salary between coworkers who joined the company at the same time can be quite shocking. For example, even if two people graduated from similar top-rated universities and joined the same company at the same time, it is possible for one of them to receive a monthly salary of 100, 300, or 1,000 yen more than the other after working there for three years. The actual difference is small; it is an amount of money that can be compensated for by not spending lavishly. But it is natural for people to be greatly shocked by it. This is something worth noting.

In the case where two people are competing for the position of section chief, when one is promoted to the position, the other will not receive the promotion. Oftentimes, the differences between them are actually very small. The reason for the selection may be that one of them is slightly more popular, a little more considerate, or has worked slightly more overtime than the other. Despite such subtle differences, as their positions change, so do their salaries and the number of subordinates they have. But even if you are the one selected in such a competition, you should not be conceited.

As in the saying "Tighten your helmet strings in the hour of victory," you need to tell yourself, "It is a serious matter that I, who am not as competent, have become the section chief over a capable rival. I'm now responsible for many people, so I have to do much better work and increase my productivity. I have to strive harder and also delegate tasks to my subordinates and help them do their work. In this way, I have to make sure that my section as a whole produces better results." Without growth in human ability, the promotion will end in failure.

If you mistakenly believe that your promotion was the result of your abilities alone, you could become the target of hostility, intense jealousy, or behind-the-scenes slander from the people around you. If the negative feelings of others grow too strong, you could inevitably be transferred to another position and be disparaged in an obvious manner because that would be the only way to satisfy the complaints.

This is similar to what happens in a democratic society. Sometimes the mass media disclose a politician's wrongdoings, such as accepting tainted money or gaining success by deception. When this happens, the politician is removed from office. The same principle more or less applies in the hierarchy of regular companies as well. Such harshness exists in this world.

I have talked about the power of basics, and it is necessary to repeatedly build on basic practices. It is important to keep disciplining yourself to be able to do ordinary tasks swiftly and accurately without burdening other people, and to open up a way to accomplish an even higher-level work.

Furthermore, you must take responsibility for any bad results you produce, and make sure not to take all the credit for yourself when you produce good results that are evaluated highly; appreciate the support and help of others and the favorable circumstances that contributed to your success. Please know that this is the secret to achieving long-lasting success.

CHAPTER TWO

Q&A SESSION

Q&A session given on October 8, 2016
at Special Lecture Hall, Happy Science, Japan

Q1

Tips on How to Constantly Build One's Power of Basics

QUESTIONER C

Thank you very much for your precious lecture today. In regard to the importance of the power of basics, which you taught us today, I understand that dedicating oneself to the basics will serve as basic training to strengthen the soul. And now, there are many things I am now determined to do.

But when I actually try to do something with consistency, I often end up giving up after a while because of my laziness, lack of motivation, or the disparity between my efforts and the evaluation of those around me. I have made repeated attempts to continue doing things that never last.

I would be grateful if you could teach us any tips on how to build the power of basics.

Willing to improve yourself is a talent in and of itself

RYUHO OKAWA

Ultimately, it has to do with one's greatness of character in a total sense. If someone cannot continue making efforts, it simply means that the person is not someone of greatness. That is because his or her aspirations are not high enough. It shows that the person has not thought deeply about the meaning of being born into this world and fails to have great ambitions that he or she wants to achieve in a life of just several decades. In this sense, even the thought of wanting to improve oneself in and of itself is a talent.

Those who become easily satisfied with their past accomplishments will not achieve further greatness. After all, it is very difficult to stay humble after having achieved success. Even sumo wrestlers sometimes get degraded after winning a championship tournament. A similar kind of demotion can happen in professional baseball. Somewhere in your heart, you need to have the willingness to go back to a mere staffer at any time, even though this is a difficult thing to do.

The difficulty of taking an English test in one's 40s

You [Questioner C] were the vice principal of the Happy Science Academy in your previous job. I do not know your age exactly; I think you are younger than me, though you do look older from that "dignified sheen" on your head [*laughs*]. While you were serving as vice principal, I remember you passed the pre-1 level Eiken English test*. I saw this when I was going over part of a report, and I was impressed by your willingness to take on a challenge.

In fact, taking the exam at your age is alone quite amazing. There are many excuses not to take the test, so it is not common for an older person to give it a try. At your current age, you might decide against taking the exam, saying that you have forgotten what you had studied, that you have a family to care for, or that you have the risk of losing face as vice principal if your score is lower than the students' scores. I understand that you would be very embarrassed if you did not pass, especially since students take the same test. The students could say, "Oh, the vice principal has also failed. Then, you can't expect us to pass either." It would be shameful indeed if the students saw that the vice principal would never be able to pass. And yet, even with all those risks, you boldly took the test and passed.

Passing the pre-1 level of the Eiken test in one's 40s is a very difficult challenge to accomplish. I have previously mentioned Mr. Yoichi Hareyama, who worked for an English language textbook publisher and was also an author himself. He wrote that he passed the pre-1 level of the Eiken test after turning 45 years old and that his friends were impressed by it. They made comments such as, "We don't think we could pass the test in our 40s. We no longer understand the questions and have no clue how to answer them; unlike in our student

---

* TF: The Eiken Test in Practical English Proficiency is an English language test conducted by a Japanese public-interest incorporated foundation, the Eiken Foundation of Japan, and backed by the Japanese Ministry of Education, Culture, Sports, Science, and Technology. Grade pre-1 is the second highest level.

days, we doubt we can understand the problems. Passing the test at your age is truly amazing."

He apparently started writing English textbooks after he took the TOEIC English test* because the people around him had encouraged him to do so. He went on to write many English study books afterward. Because he worked at a company that dealt with English learning materials, I imagine he was regularly exposed to English and probably also had opportunities to be involved in work related to entrance exam preparations as well. But he probably had never taken the test himself.

In a way, the reaction of society is honest. Working at a company that deals with English learning materials does not necessarily mean that everyone working at the company is confident enough in their own English abilities to take the tests. They are not certain whether the materials they create actually help people pass the test either; they continue to put together these materials because it is their job. But if someone making the educational materials did take the test and pass it, people would be impressed. I think Mr. Hareyama passed the pre-1 level of the Eiken test and scored over 700 points on the TOEIC test. Even with that level of proficiency, he wrote books on English study because it was already an amazing accomplishment for someone in their 40s.

---

* TF: The Test of English for International Communication (TOEIC) is an international standardized test of English language proficiency for non-native speakers. The total score ranges from 10 to 990 points.

People say that one's English ability deteriorates with age, and I really think this is true. But perhaps it has more to do with the strong feeling of embarrassment over the possible results of the test, rather than one's ability. People tend to have a strong fear of what others might say if they failed, so it is more difficult to overcome this fear than to take the test itself.

Happy Science Academy students put a lot of effort into studying English at school; some even carry English vocabulary books around with them during their breaks. So, in your case too, you may have doubted whether you could compete with such teenagers. You may have wanted to say, "I'm sure you only need to focus on memorizing a list of vocabulary words, but I have a lot of other work to do." I imagine there were a number of excuses you could make, such as, "I have administrative work to do at school. As an executive of a religious organization, I also have to study the teachings. I'm much busier than you students." I thought it was quite something that you nevertheless found time to continue studying and dared to test your abilities in a public test. It was impressive.

I believe you graduated from Waseda University, the Faculty of Political Science and Economics, but if you were to apply to the same school after 20 years had passed, normally, you would not be able to pass the exams. To be able to do so, one would have to regain the youthful spirit to study hard, but this is usually not possible. It would be even harder to focus on studying, especially if one has a wife and child at home or if the child is also studying for exams. It would be embarrassing if the child saw the study materials, so one might want to study in secret.

I am sure you nevertheless made an effort in such an environment, and I think that was amazing of you. Those who never stop making an effort no matter how old they get are great. And those who manage to achieve good results are even greater, even though I know the results are not everything that matters.

There is always a time when you have to take a leap

As I mentioned in the New York lecture ["Freedom, Justice, and Happiness," given on October 2, 2016], I was about 51 when I started studying English again. My overseas missionary work had officially started in 2007, and at the time, I was able to read and listen to English to a certain extent. But usually, such a level is not enough to give a lecture in public, and it is not easy to attain that level of English proficiency.

During my days at the trading house, there was a period when I was stationed at New York Headquarters, so I used English for work as a young man. I would speak English in meetings and when I made phone calls. Back then, I was impressed by the president of New York Headquarters, who had lived in New York for more than 20 years, confidently giving speeches in English at gatherings. Thinking back on it now, his speeches were not long and most likely lasted about 10 to 15 minutes. Even so, seeing him speak about the mindset needed for work and the future direction of the company in front of several hundred employees, which included non-Japanese staff, was quite impressive in the eyes of a young staff member; I hoped to be able to talk like that in 20 years' time.

I was not yet in such a position and did not have any opportunities to give English speeches to a large group of people at the time. I remember wishing in my 20s that I would be able to give an even more impressive speech in English when I returned as the president of New York Headquarters in two decades. Of course, this was only if I had continued to work for the company.

What actually happened after that was that I started Happy Science and officially initiated my overseas missionary work in Hawaii in 2007 when I turned 51. That year, a month before I delivered my very first English lecture in Hawaii, I had given a lecture at Tokyo Shoshinkan and expressed how I did not feel confident enough to give a lecture in English, even though I had studied English extensively for a long period of time. Despite my reservations about it, I gave an English lecture in November, one month later. So, there is a time when one must take a step forward to leap ahead.

Giving English lectures to a non-Japanese audience without a script

You can find any number of excuses for not doing something. Some executive members of our International Headquarters at the time took an interpreter with them and had the interpreter translate their Japanese into English to carry out their work. So, there were many who worked without studying English as much as I did, and I could have done the same if I wanted to.

In fact, other religious groups operate in the same way and most politicians use interpreters as well. When politicians give speeches in English, they usually have bureaucrats write or review the script and practice reading it before they speak in public.

When I went to the United States, I watched television programs like FOX television and saw that professional orators also used scripts. These people would have scripts ready before giving a speech. It is said that Martin Luther King, Jr.[*], who is famous for his "I Have a Dream" speech, would spend up to 15 hours to write a script for a Sunday sermon. He was one of the most proficient professional orators, and his speeches were of such historical importance that they are sold as CDs.

There were aspects in the speeches of former US president Mr. Obama that suggested he too had thoroughly

[*] TF: "Spiritual Interview with Martin Luther King, Jr." is available at Happy Science.

studied the speeches of people like Reverend King, Abraham Lincoln, and John F. Kennedy—he had studied the speeches of people who had spent hours writing and thoroughly checking their scripts. Mr. Obama used to hire capable speechwriters from early on, and he would read through their written scripts himself, make alterations, and practice before giving his speech.

Even those who were considered the "best orators" by other professionals gave their speeches after carefully writing full-length scripts and memorizing them. Some church ministers give sermons as they walk back and forth on the platform, but they occasionally return to the podium to look at their scripts. This is because there are times when they forget what they are supposed to say, which they fear. So, they prepare the script beforehand in case their minds go blank.

But I myself do not prepare any scripts. It may appear daring for a Japanese person to give a lecture in English without a script in front of native English speakers, but since I do not prepare any scripts when I speak to a Japanese audience, I do the same when I give a lecture in English. It entails the same level of difficulty; I read the thoughts of the audience to understand their overall level of awareness, and speak on topics that are necessary at that time, at an appropriate level and with the appropriate power for the people attending. In this way, I talk in the same way as I do to a Japanese audience. Although it may seem audacious, I do what even American professionals cannot.

There may well be many criticisms, but I do it with courage. I also continue to make basic efforts to improve my skills. I have to be strict with myself on this matter. Unless I strictly set high goals for myself, I will not be able to do this. We must not take things lightly.

Your aspiration determines who you are and what efforts to make

Americans especially have a high level of education and income compared to the rest of the world; they have economic power, have plentiful food to eat, and are extremely influential in the world. So, in a sense, we could say that each American has a level of influence that is roughly equal to that of 100 people in a developing country. Based on this thinking, a lecture to an audience of 500 people in New York could be equal to speaking to an audience of 50,000 people elsewhere.

For this reason, when I started preparing for my New York lecture about a month earlier, I was determined to study seriously and prepared as if to give a lecture to an audience of 50,000 instead of 500. Even so, my preparations were not enough. But since I approached it with the determination to put in effort to accomplish something 100 times greater than the actual target, I could only be strict with myself and remain humble, even though I may not have been able to actually put in 100 times the effort. Such an attitude is a natural requirement for a professional speaker.

If you think that a little effort will suffice because you will only be talking to a small number of people, it is not the right attitude to have. Those who have this mentality will not be able to attract a larger audience, no matter how many times they go abroad to give a lecture. Despite many attempts, their audience will not grow beyond 10 people.

The same can be said of Happy Science branch managers in Japan. I presume that some branch managers have become complacent with only 10 to 20 believers attending their lectures and see no reason to make their local branches any bigger. However, if branch managers make an effort with the wish to have more and more people come and listen to the lectures, their local branches will definitely overflow with people and start to feel small. As a result, the number of local branches will increase. If the branch managers have an even greater ability, they will be promoted to regional director or even to executive status at headquarters. This would be the natural consequence.

If branch managers think that their duty is simply to maintain the current size of the local branch, no matter how small it is, they will not make any further efforts. However, those who believe their branch should be 100 times bigger will find an infinite number of things to work on. In either case, it is ultimately a matter of one's aspirations. Your aspiration determines who you are and your greatness of character.

Therefore, if you think you lack aspiration, then you must realize that you have yet to achieve greatness. In that case, you must be humble and work diligently until you can naturally do what most other people do naturally. Do not think you can evade these matters. Even if you were a genius, like the Indian mathematician receiving formulas from a goddess, sometimes that alone is not enough to be accepted in this world. You must also study basic mathematics to convince other mathematicians and prove your ability to society. Otherwise, your talents could be wasted. After all, talent is considered talent only when it is understood and accepted by others.

In the world of professional baseball, for example, some players become so nervous in actual games that they are never able to hit home runs, even if they were knocking out plenty of them during practice with their team. As a professional baseball player, this is a problem. They may claim, "I do have the ability to hit home runs. I hit many home runs during practice and can do so as long as I am not nervous. I just cannot do it at the stadium," but it would be difficult for such players to make it as professionals.

If they cannot hit a home run during a real game because they get too nervous, they must practice until they are able to hit home runs even when they are nervous. This means they have to continue making efforts until they can exert their full potential even when they are in a disadvantaged situation.

I think this was a very humbling question.

Q2

How to Incorporate the Power of Basics

into an Organizational Culture

QUESTIONER D

Thank you very much for this valuable opportunity today. I have learned that each individual needs to practice and develop the power of basics, and that it is important not only for individuals themselves but also for organizations as a whole in accomplishing greater work.

I would like to ask your advice on how to develop the feeling of unity and harmony with other colleagues or as an organization, while each person practices the basics and pursues one's aspiration or a common organizational goal with a sense of mission.

Overcoming communication difficulties

RYUHO OKAWA

It has to do with organizational culture or corporate culture. An organizational culture is gradually established in companies that have lasted for some time. This is a natural course of events.

Toyota Motor Corporation, for example, has what is called "Toyotaism." Toyota probably has around 300,000 employees, and with that many people in the workforce, their employees probably represent the average level of the Japanese population. Since they cannot hire only exceptional people, their employees should be close to the average level of the Japanese people.

Even so, when Toyota advocated *kaizen* [the philosophy of continuous improvement], everyone started to make some kind of improvement. Having created a culture of submitting ideas for potential improvements, they annually receive more than 100,000 suggestions on things to improve. Once the regular employees adopted the spirit of *kaizen* in this way, everyone started to make suggestions. When this practice becomes the norm, all employees start to think about how to help their company move forward, even if it is just one or two steps.

Some people may think that only the top management should consider what needs to be improved. But in a large company like Toyota, even if the top executives were to give directions, their suggestions may often be inaccurate because they do not have a good understanding of the situations in the local worksites. Rather, it is the people working closer to the worksites who have a better grasp of the actual problems. If these people think that it is not their job to improve things, the problems will often get neglected and left as they are.

The chain of command tends to get longer in growing organizations, and this usually leads to the worsening of internal communication. I believe this is common in most organizations. In such companies, proper command and instructions do not sufficiently reach the lowest levels, while the setbacks and mistakes at the lower levels do not reach the top. They need to think about how to overcome this issue.

To solve this issue, all employees need to set aside their job titles, salaries, and positions in the company hierarchy, and come together to make their company better. In the same way, we need to think about how to improve the religious group Happy Science as a whole on a daily basis.

Sectionalism will lead to a drop in productivity

In my current work, I have frequently found that my disciples' work tends to be sectionalized. The term sectionalism is often used to refer to the work of government offices. They are often criticized for causing trouble by being sectionalized and uncooperative with other ministries, agencies, or departments, but their tendencies do not seem to improve.

Government officials do not undertake tasks that do not benefit their work performance or extend their efforts beyond their given roles because they could get reprimanded or assessed negatively if they fail upon giving extra assistance. Perhaps they believe that as long as they do not cause trouble, they could climb the career ladder and secure an executive position in a private-sector job after retiring from their government job. That is why they tend to avoid problems and focus only on trying not to receive negative evaluations. But this way of thinking only leads to a tremendous decline in productivity.

From my own experience, I noticed that there were different tendencies even among trading companies; some were team-oriented organizations, while others were more people-oriented. At the trading house I used to work for, although there were rules and regulations of authority which employees had to follow, work responsibilities could be expanded depending on the situation. There was a chart describing the scope of authority, the general financial responsibility, and the type of work one could handle in each position—including the president, senior executives, directors, and managers—in my desk drawer, so I had once browsed through it. But it is all about competence in trading companies, so capable people will go as far as they can. Some even take on work that is essentially handled by the president.

This of course goes against the normal rules and regulations of authority, but it could be permitted as long as the results work out for the best. For example, the company CEO residing in Japan cannot know everything that takes place in New York Headquarters. So, when someone working in the New York office sees a chance to make a beneficial deal, he or she might take a chance on a business venture. Although the deal would normally require prior permission from the CEO at the head office in Japan, the staff may decide to act on the proposal before any competitors do, and then report to the head office afterward.

In my experience at the trading house, if the decision to act without permission resulted in successfully making a profit or closing a deal, the person responsible was reprimanded for acting without permission, but would later receive an additional bonus in December. Depending on the person, the scope of authority was very flexible, which meant that each person was shouldering risks. It was as if each person were managing a company of their own, and the range of one's ability tended to differ greatly.

I used to work in such an environment. So, I am surprised when new staff at Happy Science who previously worked at jobs with clearly defined roles and responsibilities do not offer help beyond their official duties and feel okay about it.

Examples of organizations that tie responsibility and authority

There are cases where former senior officers of the Japan Self-Defense Forces become consultants and provide advice on how to manage organizations. We, too, once had such a consultant when Happy Science Headquarters moved to the Kioicho Building. He occasionally came to give us suggestions, and often advised us to grant our staff both authority and responsibility. He always instructed us to tie responsibility and authority together, making it clear that one who authorized something to be done had to be responsible for it.

I assume this is essential in the military. Soldiers are not allowed to fire their weapons until the squad leader orders them to do so, and must be in position until the leader's command to shoot. When the leader sees the approaching enemy and determines the right timing, everyone shoots all at once upon being signaled. In the military, one is not allowed to shoot at will, even if one is confident in hitting the enemy. That is why former military officers tend to tie authority and responsibility together.

Banks operate in a more or less similar manner, where responsibility always comes with authority. This is because deception and fraud can occur when handling money in business. Banks need to track down the wrongdoer when any financial inconsistencies happen, so they try to keep authority and responsibilities clear. They always separate people in charge of incoming money and those in charge of outgoing money and refunds. They make sure that one person cannot handle both.

If one person can handle both incoming and outgoing money, then it is possible for that person to cheat. The person could steal the money that comes in while making it seem as if it had been paid out. Altering accounting records would be possible in this way. To prevent this from happening, banks always have extra staff members compared to other companies. They hire more employees than are actually needed, forming an organizational structure in which a wrongdoer can be identified quickly in case of fraud.

Some companies have such a structure, but in general, I doubt that organizations function efficiently in this way.

Examples of sectionalism at Happy Science

Referring back to my own experience that I just mentioned, if I were appointed as a branch manager at Happy Science, I would probably go as far as I could with my work. Since I am that kind of person, I would think about what Master would do and keep moving forward with those ideas. After having received instruction from the regional director or the director general at headquarters, if I think, "Their directions do not align with what Master said in a recent lecture and are different from Master's ideas," I would think of how to benefit the entire organization and act based on my belief about what I have to do in light of Master's guidelines.

There was a time when I wondered why our political activities did not yield positive results, and the reason finally became clear to me in the spring of 2016, when my second son served as the director general of our Secretariat Division. One of the reasons was apparently that a lot of the activities at the regional headquarters and the local branches were focused on Happiness Planting [donations] and meeting the donation targets set by the El Cantare-Belief Promotion Division. It turns out that meeting those targets affected the assessment in deciding stipends, allowances, and promotions.

I heard a similar story from my third son when I went to Okinawa to give a lecture. Prior to my lecture, he visited one of the local branches and found that the branch manager had been cutting back his campaign activities despite running as a candidate for an upcoming election. This was because the regional director had told him to meet the target of Happiness Planting first before focusing on his political activities. When I heard this, I thought it was ridiculous. I also wondered why they were still focused on Happiness Planting when I myself was coming all the way to Okinawa to promote our political activities. According to what I heard later on, there was generally more emphasis placed on Happiness Planting at the time, so it may have been natural for the regional director to prioritize it.

In this way, these kinds of events were happening at the operational level but did not reach the top management. Sometimes there are such systemic problems. In fact, if Master encourages believers to achieve victory in political activities, the entire organization should shift its focus to achieve that end. However, a pre-established system can serve as a "lid" to hold back the organization from making this shift. I imagine there are many similar cases in other parts of the organization. This is an example of sectionalism, and a surprisingly serious case of it.

There was another case. I have heard that when new staff members are assigned to a local branch or *shoja*, they soon find that there are certain boundaries; those who work in the local branches feel that the *shoja*, or the large training facilities, are their "enemies," while those assigned to the *shoja* feel that the local branches are their "enemies." In other words, they are competing for the believers' offerings. From the perspective of Toyota's aforementioned *kaizen*, in which all employees strive to improve their company as a whole, we are at a much inferior level.

However, this is due to human nature, and the result of our limited awareness. Everyone has an ego and wants to work only within one's own circle of coworkers, without taking an interest in other matters. At the same time, people tend to see others as being below them, while wanting to raise the status of their own section, so perhaps it cannot be helped. Even so, we must change this culture to create a stronger organization.

Make sure that the organization has not become self-centered

I strove to create a unique organizational culture since starting Happy Science, but in reality, it did not work the way I intended. In fact, people who joined Happy Science from other jobs brought with them their previous corporate cultures from various industries.

It may be rather rude to say this, but the worst office culture is that of governmental offices. As an organization, the level of work at the town offices is the worst, and their productivity is the lowest. Slightly better organizations than those are companies backed by the government; they are like state-run businesses in that they have lenient ways of thinking because there is no worry of bankruptcy.

There might be some people from such organizations who have a "venture spirit" and are willing to do anything in case of a management crisis. But as an organization becomes larger, workers in general tend to become less outstanding. In a sense, this may mean that the organization has gained more stability; the fact that the organization is run by mediocre staff members means that the management has stabilized. However, there is less potential for such an organization to grow further.

In addition, there will be more people who refrain from doing their best, thinking that achieving good results this year will result in an even higher target next year. Since the targets for the next year are calculated based on the achievements of the current year, they try not to work too hard to meet the current year's target.

In the past, there was a branch manager who was reluctant to accept donations at the end of the month after having achieved his monthly target of Happiness Planting by the middle of the month. He apparently asked believers who were willing to make large donations to split them over two consecutive months because his target was already met for that month. However, this request is a very insensitive one, seen from the eyes of the people making the donations. The right timing to make a donation is the moment when a person aspires to do so. Meeting the monthly target is only the branch manager's concern. If the donations are not accepted at the right time, the believers' enthusiasm will fade and they will become discouraged.

Department stores, for example, also have their own sales targets. Each clerk is assigned a monthly and daily sales quota to meet. But when a customer wants to buy something, how would he or she feel if the clerk said, "Please come again tomorrow," simply because the sales target for the day had already been achieved? If the clerk said, "I am responsible for this sales area, and since I have already achieved my target for today, I'd be grateful if you could make your purchase tomorrow. Then I can meet my target again tomorrow," that customer would feel offended and never come back. Such service is not customer-oriented.

In my lectures on management at Happy Science, I teach the importance of putting the customer first, putting oneself in the position of others, giving love, and practicing altruism. However, we must understand that no matter how many times these things are taught, they are not often practiced in the actual workplace. That is because all of one's work has become self-centered. There are also countless cases in which the organizational work has become egocentric, which leads to a drop in the overall level of work.

Those who have a broader outlook must be promoted

So, even after establishing our political party, sectionalism still prevails at Happy Science. The number of staff involved in our political activities is less than one-twentieth of our total group. This means that only one-twentieth of our total resources are utilized to engage in political activities. Since other staff members have their own work to do, they do not take part in political activities, even if they are requested to do so. They do not participate because their performance in their own jobs is more important to them.

They probably would not listen even if I told them to do so; since they think it is not their job to help with the political activities, they do not have any intention to offer support. This will result in the isolation of each section and cause the organization to divide. In this way, we are showing tendencies of becoming an example of a bad organization, and this makes me very sad. This is the natural course that an organization will take if people are preoccupied with self-preservation.

However, there are people who can grasp the overall perspective of the organization and understand what is essential for other sections or for Happy Science as a whole. These people are management leaders, even if they currently fill lower positions, such as a senior staff member or someone without a title. People who can see the overall picture are valuable.

Those who just focus on their job performance, merely care about their assigned jobs, and only take action when instructed are no more than just "cogs in a machine." They will be used by others and will not likely progress beyond that. On the other hand, there are those who can see the whole picture and understand how the organization should move as a whole. They can envision the prosperity of the whole company as well as its influence on society, based on the consideration of other divisions and their staff members. Even if they are still young and have low status or low salaries, they are already management leaders. These people are valuable, and if these people are not promoted, the organization is bound to decline.

Of course, there may be times when you are hesitant about how far you are allowed to go, but you should do what will benefit the entire organization. You may feel dissatisfied about your work in many ways, such as being assigned too little work to do or too many miscellaneous chores, but it is important to think about the entire organization and take on other tasks if you have the energy and time to spare. If work becomes unbalanced and you are unable to complete the tasks you truly have to do, you need to speak to someone and have your workload adjusted.

So, have courage to take a step forward, and do what must be done. Even as you work in your current section, other people do not always see how much work you are getting done, so it is necessary to improve communication with others and say what needs to be said.

On the other hand, if you receive such requests or comments, it is important to humbly listen to them regardless of the age, experience level, and position of the person, and consider how to deal with what has been voiced. It is not good to just reproach the person by saying, "You are too young to say that," or to go too far and say, "Female staff does not have the right to say such things." I hope everyone remains open-minded.

Everyone must have the mindset of a business executive

If I were to talk about work as a whole, the topic would become too large to cover all the points here. But as you strive to make efforts in your current position, you will start to see more clearly what you have to do or the breakthroughs you have to make. You may also find many areas in other people's work that should not be left as is, but we must create an organization where people can back each other up. To use an example from a baseball game, if the shortstop makes an error, the second baseman or center fielder must cover for them. It is not good if all the players let the ground ball get through.

So, I ask you not to become sectionalized as a result of thinking only within the limits of your mind. There are still many sections that fail to achieve their large targets, so we all need to make decisions that will contribute positively to the entire organization. There are also many executives who have not done sufficient work and are instead making decisions that point in the opposite direction. I hope Happy Science will become the kind of organization that can change flexibly, like the body of a mollusk.

In a sense, this will help keep my work alive rather than killing it. I sometimes feel truly regretful; although I give many important teachings, I often find instances where our staff members have become satisfied in fulfilling a target they set for themselves at their own discretion. I frequently feel that we could have done better. Many people do not make additional efforts and stop halfway, which makes me sad.

Take, for example, the number of books I write. If the total annual sales remain the same whether I publish two books or 100 books a year, then writing 100 books would be a waste. Writing only two books a year would be much more efficient. However, that is not how we should think. As long as I am putting out 100 books, it means I am marketing widely to satisfy the needs of many kinds of people. I publish books on many different themes, so there must be a mission to recommend different books to people who have never noticed or taken an interest in our books before. Unless we work on this mission, the result would be the same no matter what I do. It would not go beyond the work of an individual and remain a one-man operation. Therefore, it is my hope that everyone strives to develop the mindset of a business executive.

AFTERWORD

One day before I proofread this book and wrote the Preface and Afterword, I received three of my newly printed books[*] in the evening. I was amazed by the fact that three books were published in one day. At the same time, I received a report saying that in the first half of this year, my book titled *The Laws of Mission* ranked second on the list of best-selling books according to the publication distributor, TOHAN Corporation, and first according to the Kinokuniya bookstore system. An average writer may feel envious of this publishing speed and these achievements.

But I myself do not appear particularly busy. This is exactly what is meant by *The Power of Basics and the Road to Success*. I consistently repeat the basic tasks every day, so I am always ready to receive inspiration at any time. My heart is always calm, and I intend to go far.

If, with this book, the heart of enlightenment that has been lost is successfully revived in modern times, then I am happy.

Ryuho Okawa

Master and CEO of Happy Science Group

June 3, 2017

---

[*] TF: The three books are *Haiyu Sato Takeru no Shugorei Message – Jinsei wa Tatakai da* (lit. "Spiritual Message from the Actor Takeru Sato – Life is a Fight"), *Eien naru mono o Motomete* (lit. "Seeking for Something Eternal"), and *Kokugun no Chichi Yamagata Aritomo no Gutaiteki Kokubo-ron* (lit. "On Practical National Defense by the Father of Japanese Militarism Aritomo Yamagata"), all published by IRH Press.

*This book is a compilation of the lectures,
with additions, as listed below.*

PART ONE
THE POWER OF BASICS AND
THE TIME OF SILENCE

- CHAPTER ONE -
THE POWER OF BASICS AND
THE TIME OF SILENCE

Japanese title: *Bonji Tettei to Seijaku no Jikan*
Lecture given on September 3, 2016
at Special Lecture Hall, Happy Science, Japan

- CHAPTER TWO -
Q&A SESSION ON
"THE POWER OF BASICS"

Japanese title: *Bonji Tettei ni Kansuru Q&A*
Q&A session given on September 4, 2016
at Special Lecture Hall, Happy Science, Japan

PART TWO
The Power of Basics and the Road to Success

- Chapter One -
A Lecture on "The Power of Basics"

Japanese title: *Bonji Tettei Kogi*
Lecture given on October 8, 2016
at Special Lecture Hall, Happy Science, Japan

- Chapter Two -
Q&A Session

Japanese title: *Shitsugi Outo*
Q&A session given on October 8, 2016
at Special Lecture Hall, Happy Science, Japan

ABOUT THE AUTHOR

RYUHO OKAWA was born on July 7th 1956, in Tokushima, Japan. After graduating from the University of Tokyo with a law degree, he joined a Tokyo-based trading house. While working at its New York headquarters, he studied international finance at the Graduate Center of the City University of New York. In 1981, he attained Great Enlightenment and became aware that he is El Cantare with a mission to bring salvation to all of humankind. In 1986, he established Happy Science. It now has members in over 120 countries across the world, with more than 700 local branches and temples as well as 10,000 missionary houses around the world. The total number of lectures has exceeded 3,200 (of which more than 150 are in English) and over 2,700 books (of which more than 550 are Spiritual Interview Series) have been published, many of which are translated into 31 languages. Many of the books, including *The Laws of the Sun* have become best sellers or million sellers. To date, Happy Science has produced 20 movies. The original story and original concept were given by the Executive Producer Ryuho Okawa. Recent movie titles are *The Real Exorcist* (live-action, May 2020), *Living in the Age of Miracles* (documentary, Aug. 2020), and *Twiceborn* (live-action, Oct. 2020). He has also composed the lyrics and music of over 150 songs, such as theme songs and featured songs of movies. Moreover, he is the Founder of Happy Science University and Happy Science Academy (Junior and Senior High School), Founder and President of the Happiness Realization Party, Founder and Honorary Headmaster of Happy Science Institute of Government and Management, Founder of IRH Press Co., Ltd., and the Chairperson of New Star Production Co., Ltd. and ARI Production Co., Ltd.

WHAT IS EL CANTARE?

El Cantare means "the Light of the Earth," and is the Supreme God of the Earth who has been guiding humankind since the beginning of Genesis. He is whom Jesus called Father and Muhammad called Allah. Different parts of El Cantare's core consciousness have descended to Earth in the past, once as Alpha and another as Elohim. His branch spirits, such as Shakyamuni Buddha and Hermes, have descended to Earth many times and helped to flourish many civilizations. To unite various religions and to integrate various fields of study in order to build a new civilization on Earth, a part of the core consciousness has descended to Earth as Master Ryuho Okawa.

**El Cantare,
God of the Earth**

Ra Mu
17,000 years ago

Alpha
330 million
years ago

Elohim
150 million
years ago

Shakyamuni Buddha
2,600 years ago

Thoth
12,000 years ago

Hermes
4,300 years ago

Rient Arl Croud
7,000 years ago

Ophealis
6,500 years ago

Ryuho Okawa

Alpha is a part of the core consciousness of El Cantare who descended to Earth around 330 million years ago. Alpha preached Earth's Truths to harmonize and unify Earth-born humans and space people who came from other planets.

Elohim is a part of El Cantare's core consciousness who descended to Earth around 150 million years ago. He gave wisdom, mainly on the differences of light and darkness, good and evil.

Shakyamuni Buddha was born as a prince into the Shakya Clan in India around 2,600 years ago. When he was 29 years old, he renounced the world and sought enlightenment. He later attained Great Enlightenment and founded Buddhism.

Hermes is one of the 12 Olympian gods in Greek mythology, but the spiritual Truth is that he taught the teachings of love and progress around 4,300 years ago that became the origin of the current Western civilization. He is a hero that truly existed.

Ophealis was born in Greece around 6,500 years ago and was the leader who took an expedition to as far as Egypt. He is the God of miracles, prosperity, and arts, and is known as Osiris in the Egyptian mythology.

Rient Arl Croud was born as a king of the ancient Incan Empire around 7,000 years ago and taught about the mysteries of the mind. In the heavenly world, he is responsible for the interactions that take place between various planets.

Thoth was an almighty leader who built the golden age of the Atlantic civilization around 12,000 years ago. In the Egyptian mythology, he is known as god Thoth.

Ra Mu was a leader who built the golden age of the civilization of Mu around 17,000 years ago. As a religious leader and a politician, he ruled by uniting religion and politics.

ABOUT HAPPY SCIENCE

Happy Science is a global movement that empowers individuals to find purpose and spiritual happiness and to share that happiness with their families, societies, and the world. With more than 12 million members around the world, Happy Science aims to increase awareness of spiritual truths and expand our capacity for love, compassion, and joy so that together we can create the kind of world we all wish to live in.

Activities at Happy Science are based on the Principles of Happiness (Love, Wisdom, Self-Reflection, and Progress). These principles embrace worldwide philosophies and beliefs, transcending boundaries of culture and religions.

Love teaches us to give ourselves freely without expecting anything in return; it encompasses giving, nurturing, and forgiving.

Wisdom leads us to the insights of spiritual truths, and opens us to the true meaning of life and the will of God (the universe, the highest power, Buddha).

Self-Reflection brings a mindful, nonjudgmental lens to our thoughts and actions to help us find our truest selves—the essence of our souls—and deepen our connection to the highest power. It helps us attain a clean and peaceful mind and leads us to the right life path.

Progress emphasizes the positive, dynamic aspects of our spiritual growth—actions we can take to manifest and spread happiness around the world. It's a path that not only expands our soul growth, but also furthers the collective potential of the world we live in.

PROGRAMS AND EVENTS

The doors of Happy Science are open to all. We offer a variety of programs and events, including self-exploration and self-growth programs, spiritual seminars, meditation and contemplation sessions, study groups, and book events.

Our programs are designed to:

* Deepen your understanding of your purpose and meaning in life
* Improve your relationships and increase your capacity to love unconditionally
* Attain peace of mind, decrease anxiety and stress, and feel positive
* Gain deeper insights and a broader perspective on the world
* Learn how to overcome life's challenges

    ... and much more.

*For more information, visit **happy-science.org**.*

CONTACT INFORMATION

Happy Science is a worldwide organization with faith centers around the globe. For a comprehensive list of centers, visit the worldwide directory at *__happy-science.org__*. The following are some of the many Happy Science locations:

UNITED STATES AND CANADA

New York
79 Franklin St., New York, NY 10013
Phone: 212-343-7972
Fax: 212-343-7973
Email: ny@happy-science.org
Website: happyscience-na.org

New Jersey
725 River Rd, #102B, Edgewater, NJ 07020
Phone: 201-313-0127
Fax: 201-313-0120
Email: nj@happy-science.org
Website: happyscience-na.org

Florida
5208 8th St., St. Zephyrhills, FL 33542
Phone: 813-715-0000
Fax: 813-715-0010
Email: florida@happy-science.org
Website: happyscience-na.org

Atlanta
1874 Piedmont Ave., NE Suite 360-C
Atlanta, GA 30324
Phone: 404-892-7770
Email: atlanta@happy-science.org
Website: happyscience-na.org

San Francisco
525 Clinton St.
Redwood City, CA 94062
Phone & Fax: 650-363-2777
Email: sf@happy-science.org
Website: happyscience-na.org

Los Angeles
1590 E. Del Mar Blvd., Pasadena, CA 91106
Phone: 626-395-7775
Fax: 626-395-7776
Email: la@happy-science.org
Website: happyscience-na.org

Orange County
10231 Slater Ave., #204
Fountain Valley, CA 92708
Phone: 714-745-1140
Email: oc@happy-science.org
Website: happyscience-na.org

San Diego
7841 Balboa Ave., Suite #202
San Diego, CA 92111
Phone: 626-395-7775
Fax: 626-395-7776
E-mail: sandiego@happy-science.org
Website: happyscience-na.org

Hawaii
Phone: 808-591-9772
Fax: 808-591-9776
Email: hi@happy-science.org
Website: happyscience-na.org

Kauai
3343 Kanakolu Street, Suite 5
Lihue, HI 96766, U.S.A.
Phone: 808-822-7007
Fax: 808-822-6007
Email: kauai-hi@happy-science.org
Website: kauai.happyscience-na.org

Toronto

845 The Queensway
Etobicoke ON M8Z 1N6 Canada
Phone: 1-416-901-3747
Email: toronto@happy-science.org
Website: happy-science.ca

Vancouver

#201-2607 East 49th Avenue
Vancouver, BC, V5S 1J9, Canada
Phone: 1-604-437-7735
Fax: 1-604-437-7764
Email: vancouver@happy-science.org
Website: happy-science.ca

INTERNATIONAL

Tokyo

1-6-7 Togoshi, Shinagawa
Tokyo, 142-0041 Japan
Phone: 81-3-6384-5770
Fax: 81-3-6384-5776
Email: tokyo@happy-science.org
Website: happy-science.org

Seoul

74, Sadang-ro 27-gil,
Dongjak-gu, Seoul, Korea
Phone: 82-2-3478-8777
Fax: 82-2-3478-9777
Email: korea@happy-science.org
Website: happyscience-korea.org

London

3 Margaret St.
London,W1W 8RE United Kingdom
Phone: 44-20-7323-9255
Fax: 44-20-7323-9344
Email: eu@happy-science.org
Website: happyscience-uk.org

Taipei

No. 89, Lane 155, Dunhua N. Road
Songshan District, Taipei City 105, Taiwan
Phone: 886-2-2719-9377
Fax: 886-2-2719-5570
Email: taiwan@happy-science.org
Website: happyscience-tw.org

Sydney

516 Pacific Hwy, Lane Cove North,
NSW 2066, Australia
Phone: 61-2-9411-2877
Fax: 61-2-9411-2822
Email: sydney@happy-science.org

Malaysia

No 22A, Block 2, Jalil Link Jalan Jalil Jaya 2,
Bukit Jalil 57000, Kuala Lumpur, Malaysia
Phone: 60-3-8998-7877
Fax: 60-3-8998-7977
Email: malaysia@happy-science.org
Website: happyscience.org.my

Brazil Headquarters

Rua. Domingos de Morais 1154,
Vila Mariana, Sao Paulo SP
CEP 04009-002, Brazil
Phone: 55-11-5088-3800
Fax: 55-11-5088-3806
Email: sp@happy-science.org
Website: happyscience.com.br

Nepal

Kathmandu Metropolitan City Ward
No. 15,
Ring Road, Kimdol,
Sitapaila Kathmandu, Nepal
Phone: 97-714-272931
Email: nepal@happy-science.org

Jundiai

Rua Congo, 447, Jd. Bonfiglioli
Jundiai-CEP, 13207-340
Phone: 55-11-4587-5952
Email: jundiai@happy-science.org

Uganda

Plot 877 Rubaga Road, Kampala
P.O. Box 34130, Kampala, Uganda
Phone: 256-79-4682-121
Email: uganda@happy-science.org
Website: happyscience-uganda.org

ABOUT HAPPY SCIENCE MOVIES

TWICEBORN

STORY Satoru Ichijo receives a message from the spiritual world and realizes his mission is to lead humankind to happiness. He became a successful businessman while publishing spiritual messages secretly, but the devil's temptation shakes his mind and...

13 Awards from 4 Countries!

For more information, visit __www.twicebornmovie.com__

LIVING IN THE AGE OF MIRACLES

A documentary film released in Aug. 2020

An inspirational documentary about two Japanese actors meeting people who experienced miracles in their lives. Through their quest, they find the key to working miracles and learn what "living in the age of miracles" truly means.

6 Awards from USA!

WINNER
AWARD OF MERIT
SPECIAL MENTION
IMPACT DOCS AWARDS®

GOLD AWARD
Documentary Feature
International
Independent Film Awards
Spring 2020

GOLD AWARD
Concept
International
Independent Film Awards
Spring 2020

...and more!

IMMORTAL HERO `On VOD NOW`

Based on the true story of a man whose near death experience inspires him to choose life... and change the lives of millions.

40 Awards from 9 Countries!

SPAIN
BARCELONA INTERNATIONAL FILM FESTIVAL 2019
[THE CASTELL AWARDS]

SPAIN
MADRID INTERNATIONAL FILM FESTIVAL 2019
[BEST DIRECTOR OF A FOREIGN LANGUAGE FEATURE FILM]

ITALY
FLORENCE FILM AWARDS JUL 2019
[HONORABLE MENTION: FEATURE FILM]

USA
INDIE VISIONS FILM FESTIVAL JUL 2019 [WINNER (NARRATIVE FEATURE FILM)]

ITALY
FLORENCE FILM AWARDS JUL 2019
[BEST ORIGINAL SCREENPLAY]

ITALY
DIAMOND FILM AWARDS JUL 2019
[WINNER (NARRATIVE FEATURE FILM)]

...and more!

*For more information, visit **www.immortal-hero.com***

THE REAL EXORCIST `On VOD NOW`

56 Awards from 9 Countries!

`STORY` Tokyo —the most mystical city in the world where you find spiritual spots in the most unexpected places. Sayuri works as a part time waitress at a small coffee shop "Extra" where regular customers enjoy the authentic coffee that the owner brews. Meanwhile, Sayuri uses her supernatural powers to help those who are troubled by spiritual phenomena one after another. Through her special consultations, she touches the hearts of the people and helps them by showing the truths of the invisible world.

USA
GOLD REMI AWARD
53rd WorldFest Houston International Film Festival 2020

MONACO
BEST FEATURE FILM
17th Angel Film Awards 2020
Monaco International Film Festival

BEST FEMALE ACTOR
17th Angel Film Awards 2020
Monaco International Film Festival

NIGERIA
BEST FEATURE FILM
EKO International Film Festival 2020

BEST FEMALE SUPPORTING ACTOR
17th Angel Film Awards 2020
Monaco International Film Festival

BEST SUPPORTING ACTRESS
EKO International Film Festival 2020

BEST VISUAL EFFECTS
17th Angel Film Awards 2020
Monaco International Film Festival

...and more!

*For more information, visit **www.realexorcistmovie.com***

ABOUT IRH PRESS USA

IRH Press USA Inc. was founded in 2013 as an affiliated firm of IRH Press Co., Ltd. Based in New York, the press publishes books in various categories including spirituality, religion, and self-improvement and publishes books by Ryuho Okawa, the author of over 100 million books sold worldwide. For more information, visit _okawabooks.com_.

Follow us on:

Facebook: Okawa Books **Twitter**: Okawa Books
Goodreads: Ryuho Okawa **Instagram**: OkawaBooks
Pinterest: Okawa Books

MEDIA

OKAWA BOOK CLUB

A conversation about Ryuho Okawa's titles, topics ranging from self-help, current affairs, spirituality and religions.

Available at iTune, Spotify and Amazon Music.

Apple iTune:
https://podcasts.apple.com/us/podcast/okawa-book-club/id1527893043

Spotify:
https://open.spotify.com/show/09mpgX2iJ6stVm4eBRdo2b

Amazon Music:
https://music.amazon.com/podcasts/7b759f24-ff72-4523-bfee-24f48294998f/Okawa-Book-Club

BOOKS BY RYUHO OKAWA

RYUHO OKAWA'S LAWS SERIES

The Laws Series is an annual volume of books that are mainly comprised of Ryuho Okawa's lectures on various topics that highlight principles and guidelines for the activities of Happy Science every year. *The Laws of the Sun*, the first publication of the laws series, ranked in the annual best-selling list in Japan in 1987. Since then, all of the laws series' titles have ranked in the annual best-selling list for more than two decades, setting socio-cultural trends in Japan and around the world.

The 26th Laws Series

THE LAWS OF STEEL

LIVING A LIFE OF RESILIENCE, CONFIDENCE AND PROSPERITY

Paperback • 256 pages • $16.95
ISBN: 978-1-942125-65-5

This book is a compilation of six lectures that Ryuho Okawa gave in 2018 and 2019, each containing passionate messages for us to open a brighter future. This powerful and inspiring book will not only show us the ways to achieve true happiness and prosperity, but also the ways to solve many global issues we now face. It presents us with wisdom that is based on a spiritual perspective, and a new design for our future society. Through this book, we can overcome differences in values and create a peaceful world, thereby ushering in a Golden Age.

---

*For a complete list of books, visit **okawabooks.com***

THE TRILOGY

The first three volumes of the Laws Series, *The Laws of the Sun*, *The Golden Laws*, and *The Nine Dimensions* make a trilogy that completes the basic framework of the teachings of God's Truths. *The Laws of the Sun* discusses the structure of God's Laws, *The Golden Laws* expounds on the doctrine of time, and *The Nine Dimensions* reveals the nature of space.

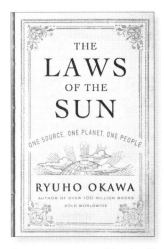

THE LAWS OF THE SUN

ONE SOURCE, ONE PLANET, ONE PEOPLE

Paperback • 288 pages • $15.95
ISBN: 978-1-942125-43-3

IMAGINE IF YOU COULD ASK GOD why He created this world and what spiritual laws He used to shape us— and everything around us. If we could understand His designs and intentions, we could discover what our goals in life should be and whether our actions move us closer to those goals or farther away.

At a young age, a spiritual calling prompted Ryuho Okawa to outline what he innately understood to be universal truths for all humankind. In *The Laws of the Sun*, Okawa outlines these laws of the universe and provides a road map for living one's life with greater purpose and meaning.

In this powerful book, Ryuho Okawa reveals the transcendent nature of consciousness and the secrets of our multidimensional universe and our place in it. By understanding the different stages of love and following the Buddhist Eightfold Path, he believes we can speed up our eternal process of development. *The Laws of the Sun* shows the way to realize true happiness—a happiness that continues from this world through the other.

*For a complete list of books, visit **okawabooks.com***

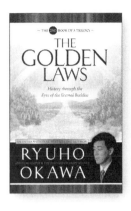

THE GOLDEN LAWS
HISTORY THROUGH THE EYES OF THE ETERNAL BUDDHA

Paperback • 201 pages • $14.95
ISBN: 978-1-941779-81-1

Throughout history, Great Guiding Spirits of Light have been present on Earth in both the East and the West at crucial points in human history to further our spiritual development. *The Golden Laws* reveals how Divine Plan has been unfolding on Earth, and outlines 5,000 years of the secret history of humankind. Once we understand the true course of history, through past, present and into the future, we cannot help but become aware of the significance of our spiritual mission in the present age.

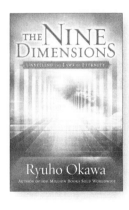

THE NINE DIMENSIONS
UNVEILING THE LAWS OF ETERNITY

Paperback • 168 pages • $15.95
ISBN: 978-0-982698-56-3

This book is a window into the mind of our loving God, who designed this world and the vast, wondrous world of our afterlife as a school with many levels through which our souls learn and grow. When the religions and cultures of the world discover the truth of their common spiritual origin, they will be inspired to accept their differences, come together under faith in God, and build an era of harmony and peaceful progress on Earth.

*For a complete list of books, visit **okawabooks.com***

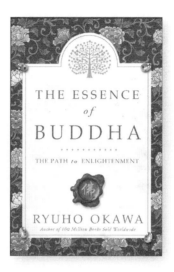

The Essence of Buddha
The Path to Enlightenment

Paperback • 208 pages • $14.95
ISBN: 978-1-942125-06-8

In this book, Ryuho Okawa imparts in simple and accessible language his wisdom about the essence of Shakyamuni Buddha's philosophy of life and enlightenment–teachings that have been inspiring people all over the world for over 2,500 years. By offering a new perspective on core Buddhist thoughts that have long been cloaked in mystique, Okawa brings these teachings to life for modern people. *The Essence of Buddha* distills a way of life that anyone can practice to achieve a life of self-growth, compassionate living, and true happiness.

*For a complete list of books, visit **okawabooks.com***

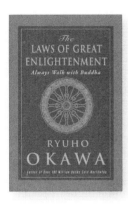

THE LAWS OF GREAT ENLIGHTENMENT
ALWAYS WALK WITH BUDDHA

Paperback • 232 pages • $17.95
ISBN: 978-1-942125-62-4

Constant self-blame for mistakes, setbacks, or failures and feelings of unforgivingness toward others are hard to overcome. Through the power of enlightenment we can learn to forgive ourselves and others, overcome life's problems, and courageously create a brighter future ourselves. *The Laws of Great Enlightenment* addresses the core problems of life that people often struggle with and offers advice on how to overcome them based on spiritual truths.

THE CHALLENGE OF THE MIND
AN ESSENTIAL GUIDE TO BUDDHA'S TEACHINGS: ZEN, KARMA AND ENLIGHTENMENT

Paperback • 208 pages • $16.95
ISBN: 978-1-942125-45-7

In this book, Ryuho Okawa explains essential Buddhist tenets and how to put these ideas into practice. Enlightenment is not just an abstract idea but one that everyone can experience to some extent. In clear but thought-provoking language, Okawa imbues new life into traditional teachings and offers a solid basis of reason and intellectual understanding to often overcomplicated Buddhist concepts. By applying these basic principles to our lives, we can direct our minds to higher ideals and create a bright future for ourselves and others.

---

*For a complete list of books, visit **okawabooks.com***

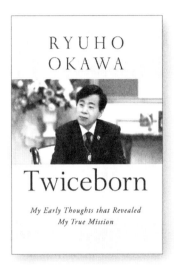

TWICEBORN

MY EARLY THOUGHTS THAT REVEALED MY TRUE MISSION

Paperback • 206 pages • $19.95
ISBN: 978-1-942125-74-7

This semi-autobiography of Ryuho Okawa reveals the origins of his thoughts and how he made up his mind to establish Happy Science to spread the Truth to the world. It also contains the very first grand lecture where he declared himself as El Cantare. The timeless wisdom in *Twiceborn* will surely inspire you and help you fulfill your mission in this lifetime.

---

*For a complete list of books, visit **okawabooks.com***

THE LAWS OF HAPPINESS
LOVE, WISDOM, SELF-REFLECTION AND PROGRESS

Paperback • 264 pages • $16.95
ISBN: 978-1-942125-70-9

This book endeavors to answer the question, "What is true happiness?" This milestone text introduces four distinct principles, based on the "Laws of Mind" and sourced from Okawa's real-world experience, to guide readers towards sustainable happiness. Okawa's four "Principles of Happiness" present an easy, yet profound framework to ground this rapidly advanced and highly competitive society. In practice, Okawa outlines pragmatic steps to revitalize our ambition to lead a happier and meaningful life.

THE NEW RESURRECTION
MY MIRACULOUS STORY OF OVERCOMING ILLNESS AND DEATH

Hardcover • 224 pages • $19.95
ISBN: 978-1-942125-64-8

The New Resurrection is an autobiographical account of an astonishing miracle experienced by author Ryuho Okawa in 2004. This event was adapted into the feature-length film *Immortal Hero*, released in Japan, the United States and Canada during the Fall of 2019. Today, Okawa lives each day with the readiness to die for the Truth and has dedicated his life to selflessly guiding faith seekers towards spiritual development and happiness. The appendix showcases a myriad of accomplishments by Okawa, chronicled after his miraculous resurrection.

*For a complete list of books, visit **okawabooks.com***

THE REAL EXORCIST
ATTAIN WISDOM TO CONQUER EVIL

Paperback • 208 pages • $16.95
ISBN:978-1-942125-67-9

This is a profound spiritual text backed by the author's nearly 40 years of real-life experience with spiritual phenomena. In it, Okawa teaches how we may discern and overcome our negative tendencies, by acquiring the right knowledge, mindset and lifestyle.

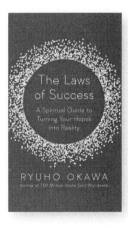

THE LAWS OF SUCCESS
A SPIRITUAL GUIDE TO TURNING YOUR HOPES INTO REALITY

Paperback • 208 pages • $15.95
ISBN: 978-1-942125-15-0

The Laws of Success offers 8 spiritual principles that, when put to practice in our day-to-day life, will help us attain lasting success and let us experience the fulfillment of living our purpose and the joy of sharing our happiness with many others. The timeless wisdom and practical steps that Ryuho Okawa offers will guide us through any difficulties and problems we may face in life, and serve as guiding principles for living a positive, constructive, and meaningful life.

*For a complete list of books, visit **okawabooks.com***

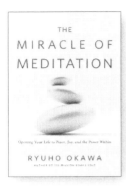

THE MIRACLE OF MEDITATION
OPENING YOUR LIFE TO PEACE, JOY, AND THE POWER WITHIN

Paperback • 207 pages • $15.95
ISBN: 978-1-942125-09-9

This book introduces various types of meditation, including calming meditation, purposeful meditation, reading meditation, reflective meditation, and meditation to communicate with heaven. Through reading and practicing meditation in this book, we can experience the miracle of meditation, which is to start living a life of peace, happiness, and success.

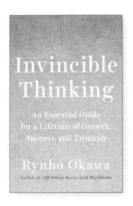

INVINCIBLE THINKING
AN ESSENTIAL GUIDE FOR A LIFETIME OF GROWTH, SUCCESS, AND TRIUMPH

Hardcover • 208 pages • $16.95
ISBN: 978-1-942125-25-9

In this book, Ryuho Okawa lays out the principles of invincible thinking that will allow us to achieve long-lasting triumph. This powerful and unique philosophy is not only about becoming successful or achieving our goal in life, but also about building the foundation of life that becomes the basis of our life-long, lasting success and happiness.

For a complete list of books, visit **_okawabooks.com_**

LOVE FOR THE FUTURE
Building One World of Freedom and Democracy Under God's Truth

THE HELL YOU NEVER KNEW
And How to Avoid Going There

WORRY-FREE LIVING
Let Go of Stress and Live in Peace and Happiness

THE STRONG MIND
The Art of Building the Inner Strength
to Overcome Life's Difficulties

THE LAWS OF INVINCIBLE LEADERSHIP
An Empowering Guide for Continuous and
Lasting Success in Business and in Life

HEALING FROM WITHIN
Life-Changing Keys to Calm, Spiritual, and Healthy Living

THINK BIG!
Be Positive and Be Brave to Achieve Your Dreams

THE HEART OF WORK
10 Keys to Living Your Calling

INVITATION TO HAPPINESS
7 Inspirations from Your Inner Angel

For a complete list of books, visit **okawabooks.com**

MUSIC BY RYUHO OKAWA

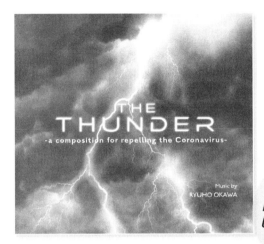

CD
available at
Happy Science
local temples

a composition for repelling the Coronavirus

We have been granted this music from our Lord. It will repel away the novel Coronavirus originated in China. Experience this magnificent powerful music.

Search on YouTube

the thunder repelling

for a short ad!

 Available online

Spotify **iTunes** **Amazon**

231

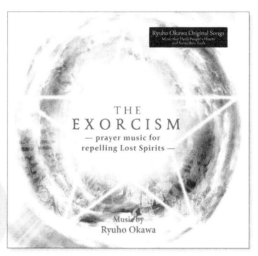

Ryuho Okawa Original Songs
Music that Heals People's Hearts
and Saves their Souls

THE
EXORCISM
— prayer music for
repelling Lost Spirits —

Music by
Ryuho Okawa

CD available at Happy Science local temples

prayer music for repelling Lost Spirits

FEEL THE DIVINE VIBRATIONS of this Japanese and Western EXORCISING SYMPHONY to Banish All Evil Possessions You Suffer from and to PURIFY YOUR SPACE!

Search on YouTube

the exorcism repelling 🔍

for a short ad!

 Available online
Spotify iTunes Amazon